Bonsai for Beginners

An Easy Guide to Caring for Your Bonsai Tree

Akira Sasaki

Introduction

Nowadays, the art of Bonsai tree cultivation is associated with Japanese culture, even though it originated in China. The Chinese called these small potted trees "penjing" which translates as "a plant in a tray." This discipline also incorporates the building of tiny landscapes and bushes in addition to cultivating trees for decoration and contemplation.

The Chinese began to keep plants in pots over one thousand years ago. The practice was quickly adopted by Chan Zen Buddhist monks, who used the process of caring for and training a Bonsai tree as a means to engender a sense of inner calm and provide a framework to ponder life's mysteries.

The practice of penjing found its way to Japan around the year 600 C.E where the it became known as "Bonsai." A "bon" is a Japanese word for a clay container commonly used to grow plants in.

The practice of growing Bonsai trees quickly become both popular and complex. Many rules were developed for properly growing, caring for and pruning these tiny trees. Growing and caring for a Bonsai was seen as a way to instill a sense of serenity in those who looked upon them and was seen as a way to take an active role in creation by shaping and pruning the tree into a beautiful work of art.

A book called "The Tale of the Hollow Tree" contains a passage which illustrates this desire to improve upon nature's beauty:

"A tree that is left growing in its natural state is a crude thing. It is only when it is kept close to human beings who fashion it with the loving care that its shape and style acquire beauty and be able to stir the emotions."

This is not some egotistical declaration of man's superiority over the natural world though it may seem as though that is the point. The Bonsai tree cultivator is nature's aid, someone who works with the tree and the environment to bring out and improve the natural beauty inherent in all creation.

The Bonsai tree was brought to the West after World War Two. The art of the Bonsai gained a boost in popularity some thirty years ago during the martial arts craze of the 1980s. Nearly everyone who lived through that time can clearly recall the image of Mr. Miyagi, the wise Karate teacher from the Karate

Kid Movies tending to his bonsai tree in between imparting wisdom to his student.

Western culture considered the Bonsai tree little more than a decoration or curio, a pleasant addition to a room that maybe inspires a feeling of calm and serenity. There is nothing inherently wrong with using Bonsai trees for purely decorative purposes, one who does so is missing out on a large part of the tradition.

There is a serenity that comes with caring for a Bonsai. There is a relationship between the grower and the tree that forms over time. This bond between plant and human becomes, after many years a friendship as equally valid and meaningful as any person to person friendship.

Some traditionalists say it takes over fifty years to become an expert in raising and training Bonsai trees, thankfully mastery isn't necessary to enjoy the many benefits of this wonderful art form.

In this small booklet, there is no way to properly convey the beauty and complexity inherent in the process of growing and caring for a Bonsai tree. In the small amount of time you spend reading this book, it is hoped you become intrigued enough to go procure a Bonsai of your own and see for yourself what this ancient practice has to offer.

Choosing a Bonsai

When choosing a Bonsai tree, there are several things to keep in mind. First and foremost among these is whether you plan to keep your Bonsai tree indoors, outdoors or both. There is no right or wrong way when it comes to where your tree is placed; it is a decision that will dictate, to some extent, how you care for you tree through the years.

The types of trees that do well indoors are Kingsville Boxwood, Ficus, Gardenia, and Serissa. Some types that like being outdoors better are Maple, Cedar, Elm, Beech, and Ginko.

If you're going to move your Bonsai tree back and forth between indoors and out, stick with a type of tree known for being hardy. Many trees in the Evergreen family are considered fine choices for indoor/outdoor growing. Your local environment is the most important factor when choosing where to grow your Bonsai.

It is also a good idea to take a look at the various species of trees and bushes that are commonly used for Bonsai cultivation and decide which type you'd like to try your hand at growing. Many common and familiar types of trees are perfectly adaptable to being Bonsai trees. Not all will be suitable to your local environment, though, so make sure you do a little research first.

Juniper is considered a good choice for many Bonsai hobbyists. This type of tree is a hardy evergreen (evergreens are a type of tree that never loses its leaves) and can survive and thrive in just about any local. It is perfectly suited to the varied climate conditions found throughout North America. It is also one of the easiest types of trees to train and cultivate. Juniper is very good at responding to the influence of the cultivator; it is easily convinced to hold just about any shape and is comfortable both indoors and out. For these reasons, it is the Juniper that is most often recommended to the beginner.

Aside from evergreens, conifers (cone-bearing, commonly needle bearing trees and bushes) and deciduous (leafy trees) families also offer many viable options. You may choose from dozens of varieties of pines, spruce, elms, oaks, Japanese Maple and many others.

Your Bonsai tree will always need access to sunlight, keep that in mind when you are choosing a spot for your tree. If you are going to grow it primarily indoors, placing it near a window will provide all the sunlight your tree could want. If you are going the outdoor route, pick a nice sunny spot so you won't have to re-position your tree too often.

How large a Bonsai tree you want to cultivate is another important factor to consider before you get started. Bonsai trees can vary in size quite drastically. Some are barely a half a foot high; some easily reach heights of around three feet. Obviously, the larger the tree, the more space it will take up. Keep in mind that a bigger tree means more of a time commitment. It also requires more of everything else- water, sunlight, space, a bigger pot, etc..

How To Grow Bonsai

Those who are about to undertake the art of bonsai must keep in mind that it is a job that requires great attention and considerable patience, along with all the stages of development and growth of your bonsai, from the first moment of cutting the roots, the choice of the pot, the shape that the bonsai will have to take.

The beginner will not be able to immediately breed an excellent quality bonsai, but he will still be able to achieve many satisfactions managing to keep the size of the chosen tree or plant considerably reduced. The starting point of the work concerns the choice between the various ways to obtain a bonsai plant that meets our needs and abilities.

There are multiple ways that bonsai can be cultivated and some techniques are slightly more complicated than others, but given the right time and patience, all of these techniques can be performed by beginner enthusiasts. You might want to try your hand at a few of these methods once you fall in love with the whole process, but you may want to pick one of these methods first and then try it out.

There are many ways to get a map that can serve our purposes; among the most common, we will remember: Bonsai taken in nature, grown from seed, multiplied by cutting, multiplied by layering, obtained by grafting, bonsai purchased in a nursery. In this order, the main rules to be observed for the best results will be listed.

In this order, the main rules to be observed for best results will be listed.

Once you're confident with that method, move onto the next. This is a continuous learning process and you will discover something new about these little pieces of art every time you work with them.

Cultivation From Seed Or Misho

If you are the type of person who loves to start things from the very beginning and if you have the patience to enjoy this entire process, then the Misho method will be very satisfying.

This is the decidedly more fascinating method as it allows the seedling to grow and to follow its development from its seed state; however, it is also the method that takes the longest time before truly embarking on the art of bonsai. Sometimes there is talk of several years.

This method involves growing your bonsai from a tree seed of your choice and although it does take a very long time, you have a hands-on experience with the entire process.

It will take a minimum of three years for a seedling to be mature enough to actually start shaping it into what you desire, but it does put you at an advantage because you have full control over your bonsai from the very beginning.
If this is the route that you would like to take, then there are several places where you can get tree seeds suitable for growing a bonsai. You can look in your surroundings or you can shop for some online. Do keep in mind that since bonsais are normal

trees, they will come from normal tree seeds. There is no such thing as bonsai seeds and some people will try and sell these "bonsai tree seeds" at a much more expensive price, where in reality you could have probably found them outside for free.

If you do choose to look in your surroundings for tree seeds, then your future bonsai will be at an immediate advantage because if those types of trees are growing naturally in your area, then you are already in the perfect environment and climate for your bonsai to thrive.

Any locally sourced seeds should be planted as soon as fall begins for the best possible results. If you are interested in growing a foreign bonsai, it will be necessary to research exactly when it will be the best time to plant the seeds. If you are interested in planting seeds that come from a different region with a different climate, then you may need to employ a stratification technique to germinate the seeds.

The seeds can be found directly in nature, which implies a good one seed knowledge or purchased from a dealer. In both cases, it is important to bear in mind that some seeds need special care before they can be planted.

Some species must be subjected to a pre-germination period in which the seeds are left for 24 hours in a basin full of water, the fertile seeds will deposit on the bottom forfeiting water, and the others will remain on the surface.

Other species must spend a cool period, between 2 and 8 degrees Celsius - 46.4 F., to be able to mature. In any case, it would be good to seek advice from a gardener who can adequately inform us about the needs of the various species of seeds.

As for seeds to buy, the packs on which the word Bonsai is written are preferred, even if any seed can become a good bonsai. But now, let's continue the job description.

After making the first decisions on the choice of seed, proceed with sowing.

The Stratification Technique

Stratification is the process of allowing seeds to germinate by simulating their natural growing conditions. Many tree seeds have the genetic programming to survive through the cold winter months in the ground and then start germinating in the spring. This enables them to maximize their chances of successfully growing into a tree and many tree seeds are only able to germinate after they've gone through a cold winter period.

Therefore, if you are planting tree seeds out of season or from different climates, it may be needed to simulate a cold season to increase the likelihood of the seeds germinating. The majority of tree species will require you to soak the seeds in water before storing them in the refrigerator for a couple of months.
Some seeds require less time in a cold climate, whereas other species may require up to three months in the cold, so it will be necessary to research this before you begin the stratification process.

Planting the Seeds

The seedbed consisting of a small container filled with poor soil, which is without fertilizers (usually a mixture of sand and peat), is prepared. In this state, the seed is already in itself wrapped in sufficient nutrients to allow it to develop well. The container should be filled up to 2 inches from the edge. The initial preparation of your pot or container will be exactly the same for planting seeds as it would be for planting cuttings or a small tree. You will first apply a layer of coarse ground like gravel or lava rock at the bottom of the container to allow for adequate drainage. If seeds sit in soil that is too wet, it will cause them to rot and they won't be able to sprout.

Once you have added the soil layer on top of the coarse layer, you can start preparing your seeds. If your seeds need to be stratified, do this first, but if you have sourced local seeds and you are planting them at the right time, then you can forgo this process.

Once the moment of sowing has arrived (usually spring), proceed by burying the seeds with light pressure, the larger ones must be covered by at least 1inch of soil, the smaller ones by 0.5 inch.

If the size of the seed is really tiny then it will be sufficient to spread it regularly. We then begin to water them abundantly and gently, taking care not to create harmful grooves in the ground.

A solution with Chinosol can also be used.
Place the seeds in a container but ensure you leave at least two inches of space between each one. As the seeds continue to grow, they will require extra space for their roots to spread. And, if the roots intertwine you may end up damaging them when you try to re-pot the individual shoots. This can hurt the bonsai's progress.

 Once the seeds are planted, another inch of bonsai soil must be added on top of the seeds and then gently compacted with your fingers. Once this is completed, water thoroughly and allow to drain. After that, don't water heavily again and only keep the soil moist until the seeds start to sprout.

Leave the seedlings alone for a year before you consider repotting. Performing this too early can put unnecessary strain on the root systems of the seedlings. Once they have been repotted, you must wait for at least another year before you consider shaping the bonsai. Even though this is a long process, it is still very satisfying to watch the little trees take form over this time.

At this point, it would be useful to cover the container with a glass or plastic bell, so as to keep the soil at a certain humidity and temperature (the ideal one is 18-20 degrees Celsius - 64.4-68 F.).

The container should be kept away from the sun, often watering the soil to prevent the seeds from drying out.

For this operation, the use of an inclined onion or a nebulizer is recommended, because, if the jet were too strong, it would move the earth and make the seeds float.

Once the seedlings are born, the bell can be removed and when the first leaves have sprouted, the transplant is carried out in a new container. It is important not to fertilize the land for at least a month.

After this period, the fertilizer will be administered in half the dose compared to that written on the pack.

When the height of the seedlings will be 4 inches, you can begin to act on the shape.

Multiplication By Layering Or Toriki

This method of cultivating bonsais is slightly more challenging but it can still be performed by a beginner if they are up to a challenge.

 The Toriki method works with air-layering and this allows for a tree or a branch of a tree to start forming new roots at a higher level because the nutrients of the existing root system have been interrupted. This sounds confusing, but sometimes a tree's trunk starts dividing into two, allowing two separate branches to grow.

Air-layering should always be done in the spring so the roots aren't exposed to extremes in temperatures and spring also maximizes the chances of roots sprouting.

This multiplication by layering consists of putting in contact a branch of the plant specially engraved with peat or earth, to make it root.

This is a method that allows you to obtain seedlings from rather large branches, in a short time, which would instead be very difficult to achieve by cutting.

The layering is recommended above all on some types of plants such as the Pomegranate, the Spruce, the Myrtle, the Maple, the Elm and the Cryptomeria, which have a great ability to develop roots both from the trunk and from the branches.

It is preferable to undertake the operation in the spring, even if good results are obtained at any time of the year. Let's see how it goes together.

There are two different methods that can be used to air-layer a tree, namely the tourniquet method and the ring method. These methods are only used on trunks that are bifurcated and one that an enthusiast can remove one of the sections and grow a new bonsai from it.

The Ring: If you are more confident and believe that you will be able to grow the roots more quickly and cut away some bark without hurting the tree, the ring method may prove to be very successful.

Once the branch of the plant has been chosen, the lateral jets are removed for a short distance and engraved in the bark, forming a ring of about 1 inch in height around which the roots will form.

Two cuts from the bottom up to the sides of the branch can also be practiced, introducing a pebble or peat into the wound so that it does not close again.

There is also a third method of practicing the wound, consisting of wrapping two very close circles of wire tightly in the established point. In this way, with the growth of the tree, the wire will cut the bark gradually.

It is also important to sprinkle the wound with rooting hormone powder and prevent it from healing.

Layering Procedure

To obtain the roots, a transparent polyethylene sleeve stops under the incision, so as to create a funnel, and it is filled with peat to wrap the wound.

The sleeve is also closed over the incision with adhesive tape and the peat is constantly moistened. If the operation is unsuccessful, the branch will wither and die after a week or two; otherwise, the roots will begin to sprout.

When the root system is thick enough (usually 6-8 weeks), the new plant can be cut under the incision, placing it definitively in a container.

When the roots have well-rooted in the pot, you can proceed with the development of the bonsai.

Trees can be quite stubborn and they won't start sprouting roots until they are forced to do so. Thus, cutting a significant ring in the bark and including root hormone will force the tree to start sprouting roots in a place where it normally wouldn't. Once the wound has been dusted with root hormone, wrap it in wet sphagnum moss and then in plastic.

The Tourniquet: It's going to take some time and preparation to be confident enough to perform this method, but the first step is to wrap a piece of copper wire very tightly around the segment that you would like to cut off from the main trunk (preferably on one of the smaller off-shoots.) You should be able to use normal copper wire for this process, but if you have a bonsai with a thick trunk or a tree with a thick type of bark, you may need to use a copper wire with a thicker circumference.

Once you have tied the wire around the segment, it's important to sprinkle some rooting hormone over the damaged bark. This hormone, along with the lack of nutrients in the trunk, will cause roots to sprout quickly because the tree is going to try and survive the trauma. After the rooting hormone is added to the wound around the wire, wrap it with wet sphagnum moss and wrap it with plastic.

This method is less extreme than the ring method because it doesn't damage the bark as severely as the ring method but it does still sprout roots fairly quickly.

The Care for These Methods: Once the moss has been tied with plastic around the wounds, it is necessary to keep the moss moist at all times. It isn't advised to drench the moss because it will hinder the root growth, but keeping it moist will accelerate the growth of the roots. It will take a few months for the bag to fill with roots, but keep the stem attached to the main trunk during this process. Only when the bag is completely filled should you remove the stem with gentle cuts and plant the roots into fertile bonsai soil.

This method is tricky, but because you can remove a section of a bonsai that is already established, you will find that this will allow for rapid growth afterward; instead of waiting four or five years before you can start shaping the tree, it may be possible to start shaping the tree in around half the time.

Propagation By Grafting Or Tsugiki

The Tsugiki method is also one of the more advanced methods and will take some practice, but just like the Toriki method, this method is also very rewarding. Translated from Japanese, Tsugiki means "to graft," and just like most other plant species, bonsais do thrive well with grafts.

Grafting two plants or trees together allows the strengths and characteristics of both plants to come through in their future development. This usually is beneficial to produce tastier fruits or more resilient plants, but grafting helps to add branches where needed and increase the foliage on a certain part of the tree. Some enthusiasts also try to combine the characteristics of two different trees that they like into one bonsai, but grafting is not an easy process and it can be risky. Without adequate practice, most grafts may be unsuccessful, so it's imperative to practice this technique on much cheaper plants and trees before you try it on a costly bonsai.

One of the most important principles of grafting is that you have to graft two trees between the same or a very similar species. Trees that are two different won't be compatible and the graft won't take. This won't only kill the graft, it might irreversibly damage the tree too. If you want to add to your bonsai, then you need to graft in branches of a species that is part of the same class or subclass.

Grafting is another way to get a bonsai plant. It consists of joining two different plants, to add their qualities into one. The plant on which the graft is practiced takes the name of "subject" or "portliness" (daiki), while the branch that is grafted is called "scion" or "grafting" (sugan: This process can be very useful for aesthetic purposes, to protect the plant from particular parasites, or to obtain a greater variety of fruit). In bonsai art, however, this method is often not recommended, especially the two types of grafting: A) *Basic grafting;* B) *Top grafting* to beginners, due to the special care and experience it requires.

The grafting is generally practiced during the spring and with very young trees, of two or three years, which manage to adapt more easily to the various situations.

Now let's see how the two main types of grafting are made: The top ones and the base ones.

Top graft: Also called ten-tsugi or Scion grafting, is made in the upper part of a plant. It is the most common sort of grafting, and it involves removing a small branch or shoot from a larger donor plant and then inserting it into another plant. With this type of graft, the end of the shoot is cut at a 45degree angle and then a similar groove is made into the receiving plant, so the shoot can fit snugly into the groove.

This technique is commonly used with juniper and pine trees, but most deciduous and evergreen trees cope very well with this type of grafting. If you have a bonsai of one of these species, you can use this grafting method to easily add extra branches or include extra foliage on the top of the tree. (The leaves on top of bonsais can seem rather sparse, so this is a way to make your bonsai seem fuller and allow for a richer look.) When these grafts are done carefully and they fit well in the beginning, there will be a little-to-no indication that there ever was a graft performed.

 It is absolutely necessary to ensure that both the donor and the receiver are both in good health. If one of the trees is in ill health, the graft won't be successful, and if there is an infection in the graft, there is a small risk of spreading it to the receiving tree. Always ensure that both trees have healthy foliage and seem very similar in stature before grafting. One of the best ways to ensure that both trees are healthy is to fertilize both trees well in the season before you are going to graft. Since grafting is best performed in early spring, it's best to fertilize regularly throughout the spring and summer months the year prior.

It's also best to protect both trees during the winter months. Frost and snow (if you are working with larger trees) can severely damage the branches and make them less likely to be grafted together. Thus, it's best to cover the branches that you want to use for grafting (it might not be possible to cover the whole tree if the tree is large, but it is possible with most bonsais).

Once you're ready to start grafting in early spring, identify which shoots you believe are most likely to join with each other. It's ideal to look for shoots that have a strong woody base and are at least 2 ½ to 4 inches long and around a ¼ inch in diameter. Don't look for any branches that are too thick because the thinner ones have a more flexible interior and have a higher probability of joining properly.

It's necessary to clean a sharp grafting knife with alcohol before cutting a shoot from the donor tree and then re-cleaning the knife before making the groove into the receiver. It may seem strange to go to this extent, but sterilizing the blade with alcohol lowers the risk of any parasites being spread between the trees.

Cut the scion with one long stroke at an angle to create a sharp point to move into the groove of the receiving tree. Since you have gone through the trouble of cleaning your knife, do not touch the cut end of the shoot with your bare hands. Contaminating the end can lessen the likelihood of acceptance.

Once you place the shoot into the receiving tree (do this as smoothly as possible as not to hurt the wood), use grafting tape to secure the branch. Wrap it around the area that you have cut and treat it like you would treat an injury on a person. Don't tie the tape too tightly because it can cut off the nutrients into the branch, but don't leave it too loose because it comes undone and the branch may not stay secured.

Ensure that the wrapping is sufficient enough to prevent water from seeping into the graft. Unlike other planting methods, you want to avoid having water seep into any graft because it can create the shoots and the scions to start to rot. You can add some plastic wrap around the tape to help with this if you are concerned about moisture or rain.

Leave the dressing on the graft throughout the winter months and watch for any new signs of life in the spring. Any new sprouts, shoots, or flowers are indicative that the graft was successful. If you see that this is starting to occur, you can slowly unwrap the dressing around the graft because the tree would have healed at this point.

Basic graft. The basic graft, or moto-tsugi, concerns instead a lateral union that is practiced at the base of the trunk or branch of a plant.

In this case, we proceed in a slightly different way: The cut of the rootstock must be practiced literally from top to bottom for the depth of about 1 inch, creating a sort of notch in the trunk.

The cut of the scion must then be studied in an appropriate way to this notch, so as to fit perfectly into the rootstock, allowing quick healing of the wound.

Also, in this case, a strong binding will be necessary to facilitate the union of the two parts. Before transplanting it is good to cut the leaves in half and cut the main root.

This will assist in welding, limiting the growth of the rootstock.

Once practiced any of the two grafts it is good to place the plant in a place sheltered from the sun and drafts, watering to keep the soil moist, but without exceeding, so as not to rot the roots. After a month, the graft should begin to throw new shoots, then the binding must be eliminated and the soil fertilized in small doses.

However, the following factors should always be kept in mind.

Plants must be compatible: It is not possible to graft two plants that have too different characteristics, such as an apple tree and an orange.

The part of the two plants that come into contact, called the change, must be carefully joined because nourishment passes from it to the upper plant. Never practice grafting in an unsuitable season, such as winter.

The direction of the buds of the scion must be the same as that of the rootstock, i.e., upwards.

A bonsai obtained by grafting, however, can begin to show good results only after a couple of years of careful care.

Bonsai Style

There are many styles to choose from when deciding on how you want your Bonsai tree to look. The most common classification of Bonsai tree styles involves separating them according to trunk shape. Traditionally there are five different ways to classify a Bonsai tree according to trunk attributes theses are:

Cascade Style (kengai style) - In this style the tree's trunk is grown to imitate a tree growing along the side of a mountain or over a body of water. The trunk of the tree is bent at an almost forty-five-degree angle to create the illusion that it is "spilling".

In many examples of this style, it appears as though a tiny tree is suspended from a bent trunk.

Formal Upright (chokkan style) - This style calls for a straight trunk or a least a mostly straight trunk. The idea here is to cultivate the Bonsai, so the trunk goes as straight up and down as possible. The top of the tree is in direct alignment with its base, and the trunk is kept as straight as possible. The branches of the tree are structured so that the thickest ones are closest to the bottom, and then they progressively get thinner and thinner as they near the top of the tree. The resulting image is very similar to a standard mental picture of a tree, one that a child would commonly draw.

Informal Upright (moyogi style) - The Informal Upright style is similar in just about every way to the Formal Upright style with one key differencethe trunk is curved a little. Not so much that the top of the Bonsai is out of alignment with the base of the tree, but enough to be different from those grown in the Formal Upright style.

Semi-Cascade (han kengai) - Similar to the full cascade, the main difference being that the tree does not dip past the top of its container.

Slant Style (shakan style) - The slant style consists of a straight trunk, like the one found in the Formal Upright style. The difference here is that the trunk doesn't grow straight up and down, it justs out of the soil at an angle. The top of the tree is off to the right or the left of its base.

In addition to the above method of classification by trunk shape, Bonsai trees are also divided into groups based on the condition of the trunk or entail growing more than one plant in the same container. Some of these styles are known as:

Forest Style (yose ue style) - This is also known as "Group Style" and is called so because it involves more than one Bonsai Tree growing in the same container.

Growing in a Rock (ishizuke style) - A fairly self-explanatory style, Growing in a Rock is just that - the tree grows out of soil placed in a crevice among a bed of rocks.

Multi Trunk (ikadabuki style) - This style features a single tree with several trunks.

Raft Style (netsuranari style) - Picture a tree that has been knocked over. Now picture that the branches on the fallen trunk are allowed to grow upright, in a way that resembles a group of trees close together.

Root over Rock (sekijoju) - Similar to the Growing in a Rock style in the sense that both involve growing trees with rocks, Root over Rock is just as it sounds - the roots of the Bonsai tree are wrapped around and grow over a rock before entering the soil.

In addition to the above classification systems, there are a few styles that defy being categorized. These are:

Broom (hokidachi style) - This is a good style for elms and other trees with wide, broom like branches. The idea is to make the tree resemble a broom. A straight trunk with the branches spreading out widely for about the top third of the tree.

Deadwood Style - Also know as Jin, Uro, Shari and many other names. This sub-style makes use of dead wood that is present on a tree. Sometimes these are referred to as "driftwood" styles.

Literati (bunjin-gi style) - This style makes use of a straight trunk with very few branches; if there is any foliage at it is near the top of the tree.

Shari (sharimiki style) - This style is meant to depict a tree that is struggling for its survival. Most of the bark is stripped off in an effort to stress the difficulties the tree is enduring.

Windswept (fukinagashi style) - A style that imitates trees subjected to high winds. It looks like it is always in the middle of a strong gust of wind. The top of its trunk is bent to create a windswept appearance from which this style gets its name.

The above styles are not absolute, many Bonsai trees will incorporate elements from more than one style. It is expected that one will mix and match elements from the different styles to bring forth their personal vision of how they want their Bonsai to look.

They should be considered as suggestions or guidelines, not hard and fast rules that need to be clung to. These classification systems are more important during Bonsai competitions, exhibitions, and as a way for Bonsai tree cultivators to exchange ideas and easily converse about their experiences - not immutable laws for growing miniature trees.

Aside from dividing Bonsai trees into groups based on their shape and condition, size is also used to differentiate different groups and subgroups of Bonsai. This chart illustrates the system of grouping Bonsai Trees by size:

Large Bonsai Trees:

- Imperial Bonsai
- Hachi-uye
- Dai
- Omono

Medium Bonsai Trees:

- Chiu

- Chumono

- Katade-mochi

Miniature Bonsai Trees:

- Komono

- Shohin

- Mame

- Shito

- Keshitsubo

After you have procured your tree, seeds or cutting, a pot and have decided on which style you'd like to make a go at, you are ready to prepare or plant your Bonsai. In the next chapter, we will discuss what's involved with the initial planting and caring for your Bonsai.

Group Styles

Growing bonsai can be rather addictive and as you become more and more confident with certain skills, you might feel like you would like to expand your expertise to a greater level. Having group styles and more than one tree in one container is a great way to start moving into more advanced levels. Let's now consider those styles that are suitable for groups of bonsai, both those grown from the same root, and those grouped together.

According to Japanese bonsai rules, there should never be a pan number of plants, except for number two.

Sokan or style of the twin trunks- The double and triple-trunk feature (Sokan and Sankan) is common in trees in nature, but it is rather rare to see it as a bonsai.

This style concerns two trees grown from the same root. It happens for trunks that sprout from the same root system, but because of the confined space, it is rare for bonsai to be able to do this. But when this does happen, the two or three or trunks will vary in length, thickness, and how many branches they produce.

The thicker and most developed trunk will grow upright with one or two other trunks growing outward, but all of the trunks will contribute toward the foliage to make a complete canopy in the years to come.

This isn't necessarily a technique that one can force onto their bonsai and although it can happen naturally, it will require a few extra precautions when repotting these types of bonsais. The roots may intertwine and be very delicate closer to the trunks and damaging them may irreversibly hurt the tree. Thus, take extra care when dealing with these types of bonsai.

The tree that has a more robust trunk is usually called the father, the other son.

The point where the two trees join the root must be as low as possible, so as to give the impression that the bonsai is a composition of two completely autonomous plants.

Sankan or triple trunk style - This style is a variant of the previous one since three twin trees branch off from the root, which must have different sizes to recognize a father, the largest, the son, the minor, and the mother, the one intermediate.

Again, the conjunction with the root should be as low as possible.

Kabudachi or multiple trunk styles – The Kabadachi style is very similar to Sokan and Sankan because it refers to a tree with multiple trunks but they all come from the same root system. Yose-ue, on the other hand, is slightly different because it is the forest form of bonsai collections.

This is arguably one of the most complicated and advanced forms of keeping bonsai because it not only takes patience, it also takes a remarkably gentle hand and significant experience. In these designs, the larger trees are arranged in the middle of the display with the smaller ones on the outskirts to resemble a real forest. These can be grown from seedlings and nurtured and styled in the same container, or you can move more mature trees into one display. But caution is needed here because the roots of the trees will intertwine and they will be easily damaged. Thus, you will need the help of a few people if you ever had to move the forest bonsai into a larger container so the roots aren't overly damaged.

Always starting as a base from the Sokan, in this style trees are left to grow from the roots in any odd number greater than three, so as to form a small forest.

It is also necessary to remember for this style the importance of the conjunction of plants with roots.

Ikadabuchi or raft style - According to this style, the tree looks like it has fallen to one side and has begun to root downwards and branch upwards, creating new stems that arise from the ground.

For this style, it is better to choose a plant with many branches on one side of the trunk, by cutting or directing the other branches in the right way.

The main trunk must be arranged horizontally and partially covered with earth, making all the branches come out vertically.

As the months go by, new roots will grow in the lower part of the trunk and it will become necessary to cut the original roots of the tree which, until then, were arranged horizontally.

There are also options of growing groups of bonsai on larger pieces of wood, which is known as the raft bonsai style or Ikadabuki. This method is effective because either the wood will start to degrade and give extra nutrients to the bonsai, or the bonsai will find the roots of the wood and start joining their roots with theirs. The conjoining of roots allows for multiple bonsai to grow together with the piece of wood. This method is very successful in group styles because it is less likely for the bonsai to lack nutrients, unlike in rocky terrains, which are far riskier.

Group styles are normally more advanced, but there is no reason for you not to try your hand at some of these styles. Once your confidence has grown in managing single bonsais, you will manage group styles fairly easily.

Netsuranari or sinuous raft style - It is a style that derives from the previous one, from which it differs only for a small feature.

In fact, the trunk of the tree, always arranged horizontally, twists on itself, giving the whole bonsai a sinuous effect.

Yose-ue or forest style -The Yose-ue style refers to the composition of several trees of the same species, but of different ages and sizes, so as to form a miniature forest.

This style requires special preparation and care as, for a good aesthetic result, both spaces and the arrangement of plants must be carefully dosed.

However, it is possible to define some rules that facilitate the composition.

- First of all, it is good to keep in mind already from which angle you want the bonsai to be observed.
  It is therefore recommended to prepare an approximate drawing of the desired arrangement, so as to study the way to prevent two plants from being covered by each other.
- Usually, the trees are arranged in decreasing order of height: In the foreground the larger ones, the medium ones in the center, and at the bottom the smaller ones.
  This is to give the overall composition a greater three-dimensional effect.

-   Always keep in mind that even the empty spaces between
    the trees have great importance for the harmony of the
    image.

Great importance also assumes the preparation of the pot in
which the bonsai will be planted. This must have a narrow
edge and be elongated in shape, large enough to allow each tree
adequate root space.

On the bottom of the container, it is necessary to place a wire
mesh with tight links, carefully covered with the first layer of
gravel and a subsequent layer of bonsai soil.

After arranging the trees, add more soil to the empty spaces
and press it carefully.

Starting Your Bonsai

How you start your Bonsai tree depends entirely on whether
you are working with seeds, cuttings or a young purchased tree.

Preparing a Finished or Near Finished Bonsai Tree

If you have obtained a growing or already grown Bonsai tree,
all you need to do is re-pot it. Transplanting a Bonsai tree from

one pot to another is a relatively simple process for you and a dreadful affair for your Bonsai Tree.

It is a stressful ordeal for a tree to be uprooted, moved to a different location and replanted. After you are done, it will take the tree a few weeks to adjust to its new home. During this time, make sure it receives extra attention from you. It should be placed in a spot where it will not be disturbed, given extra water and allowed to settle in.

Spring is a good time to transfer a tree to a new space. Spring is when many types of trees exit their dormant winter stage and are ready to begin growing again.

To transfer your Bonsai tree from one spot to another, follow these steps:

1. Cut back on watering your tree a few days before the transfer. Dry soil iseasier to remove from the tree's roots.

2. Prepare your new pot beforehand to cut down on the amount of time thetree is not in soil. You may want to cover the drainage holes in your pot with a mesh wire. This will help prevent soil loss while still allowing for water to drain. Bonsai

trees are usually planted in a fast draining soil, making soil erosion an issue.

Place a layer of coarse dirt at the bottom of the pot and add your growing soil on top of this base layer. Don't use regular gardening or potting soil. Bonsai trees require a certain mixture of elements in their soil that is different from what other types of commonly grown plants need. More information about soil is found at the end of this chapter.

Make sure you leave enough room in your pot for your Bonsai's roots to be covered up by soil. Not much space is required; you want the trees roots to be near the surface of the pot. Typically one or two inches should be sufficient. It varies from tree to tree, and it is usually a simple matter to determine the proper amount.

3.   Take the plant out of the pot it is residing in. Be gentle and take care not todamage the roots. Clear away as much dirt as you can, you want to be able to clearly see the roots.

4.   Prune the roots. Cut the larger, thicker roots and rid the plant of any upturned roots. You want the roots to be thin, and rather long that will stay near the top of the soil.

5.   Place the Tree in its new home. Cover the roots with more soil, make surethey are entirely covered. Some Bonsai growers like to place a layer of moss or some tiny rocks on top of this final layer of soil. Not only does this practice improve the aesthetic appeal of the plant, but it also helps the roots stay secure.

6.   If the Bonsai doesn't seem stable in the new pot, run a length of copperwire through the drainage holes and gently wrap it around the trunk of the tree to help stabilize it. Your Bonsai will take a little over two weeks to fully adjust to its new digs. Make sure you follow the instructions presented earlier to ensure a successful re-potting experience.

Working With a Cutting

When starting a Bonsai tree from a cutting, prepare the pot as you would in the re-potting example, but fill the pot almost to the top with potting soil. There is no need to leave room for a root system because there isn't one yet.

Remove the leaves from one end of your cutting and cut the end on a slant. Pace the cuttings in the soil, about halfway and water thoroughly. For the next few weeks make sure that the soil is damp, but not too wet. Follow the guidelines for caring for a recently transferred plant and with some luck, your cutting will take root and begin to grow into a proper Bonsai of its own.

If all goes well, in about two years, your cutting will be ready to train, or shape.

Growing From Seed

This is the most time-intensive and difficult way to start a Bonsai tree. Aside from the amount of time you have to wait before it is ready to train and prune, growing a tree requires much more time and effort than many are willing to give. If you want to try growing a Bonsai tree from seed, consider starting the tree as you would any other plant. Research the species of tree you want to grow and make sure you can meet its requirements. Your young tree will most likely be spending its formative years indoors, and this will require the ability to duplicate, it's natural environmental conditions. Depending on your location and the type of tree you are growing, you'll need to be able to control the internal temperature and lighting in addition to several other factors.

No Matter which method of starting your tree you choose, there are several things that need to be paid attention to no matter what. Each species of tree will require different standards of care and attention from you. Some of the most important contributing factors to the success of your Bonsai are:

Location - as previously stated, think ahead about whether you want to keep your tree inside or out. Traditionally in Japan Bonsai are grown indoors, but you shouldn't let tradition stop you.
Indoor Bonsai growing is both popular and necessary for those who live in less than ideal climates for outdoor growing.

Soil - Bonsai trees require a different kind of soil than most plants. A common soil mixture consists of thirty percent pumice and 70 percent what is known as "Akadama soil" This is a special type of clay based soil that is native to Japan. While it is possible to mix your own Bonsai soil, it is much easier to buy a ready made batch from a Bonsai dealer. A few minutes of internet research will turn up more than a few reputable supply houses.

Access to Sunlight - All trees and plants need copious amounts of sunlight. It is your job to provide your Bonsai tree with enough light. Usually, indoors, it is enough to place the tree near a sunny window. If you are unable to supply your Bonsai with natural sunlight, consider the use of a grow light.

Tools - There are many specialized tools that are meant to make caring for and pruning Bonsai trees as easy a process as possible. While it is nice to have specialized tools specifically for tending to Bonsai, they are often expensive and very similar to standard gardening tools. A nice pair of shears is recommended and a set of miniature basic gardening tools should suffice the beginner just fine.

You'll also want some copper wire, as this is used to wrap around the trunk and branches to help establish the Bonsai tree's shape.

The wire is used to hold the tree the way you want it. When coiling the wire around the trunk and branches of your tree, make sure you don't tighten it up too much - otherwise it will bite into the tree and cause damage.

If you purchased a tree and have had only to re-pot it, you are ready to care for and shape your Bonsai. You should have already decided on a style by now and can begin the process of wiring your tree to hold it's shape. After the shape is established only routine maintenance and pruning are required.

The thing that makes a Bonsai different than other plants is how it is treated, not so much how it is grown. Before we part ways, we will briefly discuss the proper attitude of the Bonsai cultivator.

Bonsai Tools

Let's now describe the main tools to be used in the maintenance and transformation of bonsai. For those who are preparing to start growing a bonsai, the following tools are needed:

1. A plastic or metal watering can equip with replaceable onions with a flat and inclined face. The first

provides a strong enough jet, useful for watering leaves and foliage. The second is to be used to water the soil as it makes the water flow more gently.

2. A pair of elongated bonsai pruning shears. The length of these elongated allows you to work inside the foliage very easily.

3. A pair of wide scissors, useful for truncating large roots. A bonsai hacksaw can also be used for this purpose.

4. A pair of concave shears, useful for cutting branches to obtain a section as regular as possible, facilitating wound healing.

5. Mesh in thin mesh to be placed over the drainage holes, to prevent lumps of earth from coming out.

6. Aluminum wire to wrap branches and trunk, in case you want to change its shape.

7. A small wire cutter to cut the wire without injuring the bark.

8. A stick or a paperclip to clean the roots from the ground and separate them during repotting.

9. A rake to level the ground.

10. A broom to clean.

It is essential to remember to carefully clean each tool after use to avoid the spread of germs or diseases. For this purpose, it is possible to find types of disinfectants for tools on the market.

Proper Watering of Bonsai Trees

Proper watering is essential to promote robust growth in the bonsai. Watering should be done at the appropriate times and in adequate amounts. When and how much water depends on factors such as the type of bonsai (tree species), weather, season or climate, the size of the bonsai tree, type of soil, and the size of the pot. The numerous factors make it nearly impossible to establish a definite watering rule. What is available is guidelines on how to determine how much water and how often. All it takes is careful and frequent observation for bonsai care and maintenance needs.

Frequency of Watering Bonsai

There are lots of factors to consider when determining how often to water bonsai trees. There isn't any hard and fast rule. It will always depend on how the trees look. If they look as if they need watering, then water. But what to look for?

Check that the soil has gotten slightly dry

Never wait for the soil to get too dry before watering. Regularly check the dampness of the soil. If it looks and feels slightly dry, then it's time to water. Sometimes it will be more frequent if the soil is porous (with higher drainage), when the weather is hot (e.g., summer days), or when the tree is in a growth spurt, etc.

Feel the soil. If it feels wet, do not water. When checking, get a few soil samples about 1 cm (or 0.4 inches) deep. Seasoned gardeners and bonsai growers can tell if the soil is still wet or slightly dry just by the looks of it, without having to feel it.

Never follow a watering routine

It is best to water based on need rather than on a schedule. Water consumption of the tree and the rate of soil drying vary, based on various factors. These factors vary the frequency of watering. Hence, following a routine is likely to result in over- or under-watering. Observe the trees individually to check for individual watering needs.

Choose the right soil mixture for the bonsai trees

Different tree species require different growing conditions, including soil types. Check what type of soil the chosen tree species thrive best. Also, the type of soil contributes to how often to water. Soil types with poor drainage tend to retain water for a longer period compared to soil types with good or fast drainage. For example, clay and clay-based soils tend to hold water, requiring less frequent watering. Soils that have less capacity for holding water will allow more water to drain or flow out. These soil types will require more frequent watering.

Traditionally, bonsai trees are planted in a soil mix composed of akadama, potting compost, and fine gravel. The ratio is generally ½ akadama to ¼ fine gravel and ¼ potting compost. This has moderate drainage. If checking the soil and watering the trees regularly is not possible due to a busy lifestyle, then, create a soil mixture that can hold more water for a longer period. One example is to add more potting compost to the soil mixture.

When to water

The time of day when to water is not that very important. The most important thing is to water frequently before the soil gets too dry. Although, some bonsai enthusiasts have bonsai experts advise against watering in the afternoons using cold water, especially when the bonsai was exposed to the warm sun all day. The soil would rapidly cool down when doused with cold water. The rapid temperature change may cause some growth problems to sensitive tree species. This may cause the leaves to wrinkle or wither sooner. Growth may delay or flowering becomes poor. However, this all depends on what tree species is being cared for. Best to check the specific care and watering instructions for the chosen bonsai tree species.

In general, it does not really matter much what time of the day to water. Just water around the base of the trunk as soon as the soil feels slightly dry.

How to water

When watering, thoroughly soak the soil and the roots. Water enough so that the bonsai's root system is completely wet. Pour water at the base of the trunk until water flows through the drainage holes of the pot. Stop and allow the water to soak into the soil and the roots. Repeat this process after a few minutes.

To avoid washing away the soil during watering, use a watering can. The nozzle should be fine so that the flowing water won't be too heavy. Water from above. However, some gardeners do not recommend watering from the top of the leaves, especially in hot climates because it may cause the leaves to scorch. Check with the watering requirements for each species for the best guidance.

The best water for great bonsai growth is rainwater. Collect rainwater and store in covered containers. Then use whenever the bonsai needs watering. Some use freshwater from springs or ponds. These are the best water for use on bonsai trees because there are no added artificial chemicals. These are also rich in natural minerals that aid in better and more robust growth. If not available, bonsai will still thrive well when watered with normal tap water. However, those who want the most natural and organic growth try to avoid chlorinated water.

Fertilizing Bonsai Trees

Fertilizing is adding more plant food to support growth. This is very important during the growth season to maximize growth potential. Adding fertilizers at the right time supports strong, sturdy trunks, healthy branches, and bright foliage. Bonsai roots have a limited area to expand and search for food. Whatever nutrients present in the soil can be quickly used up. To keep the bonsai adequately nourished, adding fertilizers is vital.

Basic Fertilizer Components

Fertilizers contain the 3 basic compounds nitrogen (N), potassium (K) and phosphorus (P). Each of these elements serves specific purposes in plant growth. Nitrogen supports the growth of the stems and leaves. Potassium supports the growth and development of flowers and fruits. Phosphorus supports the healthy growth of the root system.

Fertilizers come in various ratios of these elements. And each ratio is used at certain times of the year, depending on season and stage of growth.

When to fertilize

The best time to fertilize is during the bonsai tree's growth season. Apply the right ration during the entire growth period, which is usually from early spring until the middle of autumn. Bonsai trees grown indoors can be fertilized throughout the year.

Fertilizing may do more harm than good in some instances. When a bonsai tree is repotted, most experts agree not to fertilize for a month. Allow the roots to establish themselves well first in the new environment before giving them any fertilizers. Also, when a tree is sick, postpone the application of fertilizers. The concentration may be too much for the tree to handle and worsen the condition.

To maximize growth, the right kind of fertilizer should be used at the right time. During the early spring, the best fertilizer to use on bonsai trees would be one that has a relatively high concentration of nitrogen, such as NPK 12:6:6. This is best for boosting bonsai tree growth. In the summer season, the best fertilizer is one with a balanced ratio of NPK, such as NPK 10:10:10. In the autumn, the fertilizer should help harden the bonsai for the winter season. An example is NPK 3:10:10.

Aside from growth, different types of fertilizers are also given to the bonsai trees to promote certain traits or support certain plant development. For example, a fertilizer like NPK 6:6:12 applied to bonsai trees encourages flowering. Older bonsai trees would thrive better with fertilizers that have lower nitrogen concentrations. Or, just use the same ratio but in fewer quantities.

Fertilizers are basically the same. Regular fertilizers used for gardening can be used safely on bonsai trees. Just make sure that the ratio used is right for the season and the tree growth stage. Solid or liquid fertilizers are totally fine. It's best to use fertilizer covers when choosing to use solid fertilizers. These covers will help keep the fertilizer in place and be used by the plant. Follow closely the application guidelines on the packaging of the chosen fertilizer.

When applying fertilizers, follow the recommendations on the packaging. However, reduce the amounts slightly when applying fertilizers to bonsai trees that are no longer being trained. Fertilizing at this point is for balancing growth and not for stimulating it. Avoid applying too much fertilizer and stick to the directions for use. Overfeeding does more harm than good. Giving too much fertilizer will not make the bonsai tree grow faster or bigger over a shorter period. Sometimes, it will cause stunted growth, wilting, and even death.

Pruning

One of the most important ways to make your bonsai grow in the way that you want it to is to prune it on a semi-regular basis.

Pruning, in fact, is the main job that allows us to keep a small tree, as it gives us the opportunity to modify and control the natural plant development.

By cutting a branch, in fact, it is prevented from continuing to grow and forces them to develop small sub-branches that will form a 10 crown.

However, it is good to consider that there are different ways of pruning depending on the style and the type of tree you want to grow.

There are two different types of pruning techniques that are needed: maintenance pruning, which refines and maintains the structure of the bonsai; and structural pruning, which is more aggressive but gives the bonsai a more basic or natural style. Before knowing the difference between these two techniques, it is important to fully understand how trees grow and act within their natural environment. Understanding how trees grow and why they respond to certain conditions will help you prune them effectively.

Trees, naturally, have a tendency toward apical dominance, which means their trunks will almost always grow bigger and stronger than their side stems and other offshoots. And this dominance carries on throughout the entire tree. The main trunk has smaller branches, but those smaller branches will be dominant over other smaller branches. This sequence carries on until only the foliage is left.

This is a natural mechanism that many trees have to grow taller instead of casting shade over other trees next to them. But this apical dominance also causes the tree to keep distributing growth to the top and outer branches and this ultimately causes the inner branches to die. This is normal in nature, but it can be aesthetically unpleasing to the eye in the world of growing bonsais.

Once an enthusiast knows the natural growth patterns of a tree, they are able to use pruning techniques to counter the negative aesthetic effects of apical dominance. Since dominant growth occurs in a tree's trunk, it's easy to surmise that the top and outer portions of the bonsai should be pruned more thoroughly. This pruning forces the tree to redistribute growth to the inner and lower parts of the tree, which gives the enthusiast control over the growth of the tree, the thickness of the trunk, and the overall aesthetics of the bonsai.

Structural Pruning

If you have grown your bonsai from a seed/seedling and you have waited for a few years for it to get to the place where you can start pruning it, there will come a time where the tree is strong enough to be pruned and shaped according to what you would like. Structural pruning involves removing larger branches from your bonsai and shaping it into the tree that you want it to be. But, this is a rather stressful process for most enthusiasts because even though the large branches will grow back, the first structural pruning will determine the growth pattern and the overall look of the bonsai. Therefore, it's necessary to carefully consider what type of style you would like for your bonsai. Do take into consideration what species of tree you are growing and what styles suit it. Once you have considered the style and decided on the right one, carefully consider which branches would need to be pruned to start the process of the style.

Because these prunings are rather traumatic on the bonsai, it's better to rather perform them in early spring or late autumn. This enables the bonsai to either enter or exit a growing season. Both of these are normally successful, but if your species of bonsai doesn't cope well in cold weather, it will be better not to prune it in late autumn because the tree will have the combination of cold weather and the trauma of pruning which may kill it.

To start this type of pruning, place your bonsai on a table and look at it from eye level. Start by removing all of the dead foliage and branches from the tree. Once that is completed, start analyzing the bonsai and decide which larger branches you want to remove. This includes all of the branches that block the view of the main trunk, branches that cross over with each other, and disproportionately thick branches at the top of the bonsai.

It is an unfortunate fact that pruning thick branches will leave scarring on the bonsai but this can be reduced if you use concave bonsai cutters. Since your bonsai is an aesthetic work of art, it is worth investing in these types of cutters to reduce the effects of scarring and keep the bonsai as pristine as possible.

If your bonsai is healthy, you can safely remove up to ⅓ of its foliage (which is the same percentage of roots you are allowed to prune before putting your bonsai in danger), but this type of "big" maintenance should only be performed once a year. Anything more can, and most likely will, damage your tree and cause it to die prematurely.

Before embarking on the pruning operation, you must have a clear understanding of the shape you want to give the plant so that you know where to start.

We take the appropriate tools, such as simple bonsai and bud shears, and get to work, remembering some basic rules, which are indispensable for obtaining the necessary effects of harmony and balance.

First of all, the branches must not grow in the lower part of the trunk.

Usually, the branches are started to develop at a third of the total length of the trunk, to give the plant greater impetus.

It is important to take into great consideration the point where the plant is observed; in this way, it will be evident, as we have seen, that the branches that grow on the front of the plant are useless, while those on the sides and on the back will be accentuated.

To give a livelier image to the bonsai, while maintaining a harmonious appearance, it is good to avoid the branches that grow at the same height and parallel, and also, during pruning, remember not to prune all the branches to the same size, but to leave different lengths.

If you want to limit the growth of a branch, to keep it small, it is sufficient to trim it, otherwise, it will develop and strengthen.

It is advisable to carry out pruning in the period of the year in which the crown is developed, so as to have undergone a clear image of the cuts that are being practiced on the bonsai.

Finally, it is very important, when you want to cut a whole branch, as close as possible to the trunk, by leveling the cut, so as to hide the wound from sight.

For this purpose, the use of concave shears is recommended.

In addition, in the case of particularly deep wounds, it is good to use a suitable disinfectant to be purchased from a nurseryman.

Sometimes to give an older image to the bonsai, a special tool is used, called a jinning forceps.

This allows the branches to be cut so as to leave part of the bark of the branch attached to the trunk, giving the impression that the tree has been affected by lightning.

For use of pruning to direct the growth of branches. By pruning the branch, a just above a bud facing downwards we will obtain a branch that will grow upwards after drawing a curve.

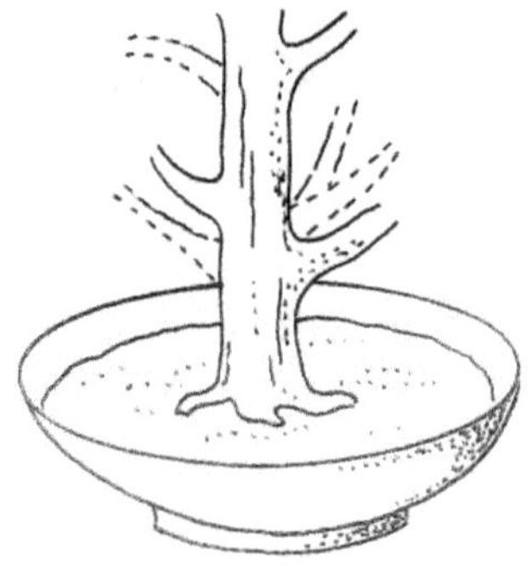 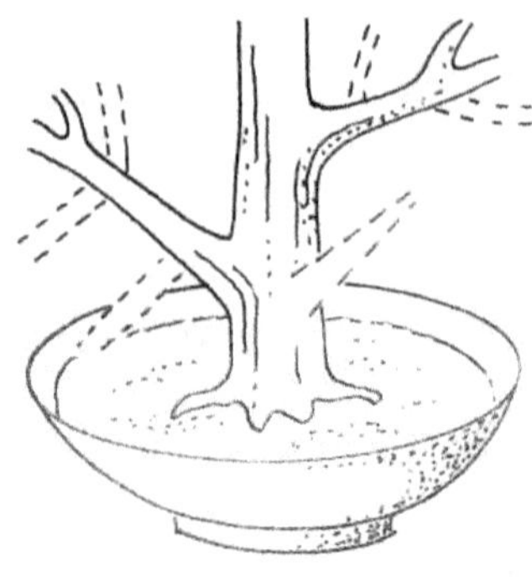

The dashes in the two sequences, show the branches that are of no use for the formation of any bonsai style, therefore they must be pruned

How to trim the shoots of a conifer

This technique is particularly difficult and still requires some experience in order not to ruin the plant.

Finally, it's advisable to do some shopping online and purchase a cut-paste that you can apply to all of the wounds on the bonsai after pruning. Infections in trees aren't uncommon and if you have spent a lot of time and effort on your bonsai, the last thing you want to do is lose it because of a bad cut. Bonsai cut-pastes prevent infections and promote faster healing.

Maintenance Pruning

The primary goal of maintenance pruning is to prevent a bonsai from acting as it would in nature. Once a tree starts to focus its growth towards the top and outer branches, the bonsai doesn't really look pleasing to the eye any longer. So, maintenance pruning needs to be employed on a regular basis to keep it from growing in areas where it isn't supposed to. When those areas are pruned away, the tree naturally sends the nutrients to the trunk and starts to increase in size centrally — this results in a much better-looking bonsai.

If you are unsure when to prune your bonsai, it depends on whether you keep your bonsai outdoors or indoors. Outdoor bonsais should only be pruned during the growing seasons of spring and summer. Since the cold makes the tree go dormant and doesn't send a lot of nutrients to the foliage, it's redundant to prune during the cold months. But, if you have an indoor bonsai, you can prune all-year-round because the bonsai will remain warmer inside and, thus, not have a dormant period.

Unlike pruning rose bushes, you don't need to excessively prune your bonsai when you're maintaining its shape. Only prune the areas that start growing too quickly. If a branch becomes too long or the canopy is uneven, then snip those parts off.

Use sharp scissors to snip away at the branches and maintain the leaves, but if you have a pine or another coniferous bonsai, it's better to rather pinch the branches off with your fingers because snipping it with scissors can lead to unsightly brown discolorations and dead foliage at the pruning sites. Since the bonsai is still small, the branches are tender enough to easily be pinched off by hand.

Some bonsais are better pruned with scissors, while others are better pruned with your fingers, but some actually need a combination of the two depending on the type of tree and strength of the branches. Hence, adequate research on your bonsai is necessary to know exactly what is the best method of maintenance pruning.

Cutting Leaves And Buds

It happens that an indoor bonsai throws the buds all year round, so pruning leaves and buds are an almost daily practice.

However, it is easy to apply, in fact, the rules to follow are less numerous than for pruning branches.

The important thing is to remember that where a sprout is left there, a branch will develop, while the lower part of the trunk will be strengthened and the branching will become thinner.

In any case, it is good to remember that the leaves must always be cut leaving a piece of a stalk and that the direction of the last leaf a stalk left after cutting also determines the direction of the bud that will grow later.

It is recommended to always cut the biggest leaves. As for the plants that bloom, pruning will only be done after the development of the flowers.

While for subtropical plants the right period for cutting shoots and leaves is between spring and autumn, tropical plants, which grow all year round, will always be pruned and pruned.

In conifers, the topping of the shoots, an operation sometimes performed simply with the nails, will cause many small needles to develop. In short, the cutting of the leaves allows us to obtain three main results: A thin branching, the shrinking of the leaves and greater ventilation of the crown of the branches.

Every year, in the period between March and August, it is good to proceed with the total defoliation of the tree; in doing so, the plant is stimulated to develop new shoots in a short time, accelerating vegetative growth.

Smaller leaves and thinner branches will grow under the petioles, giving the bonsai the classic appearance of a dwarf tree.

Effects of leaf pruning

Soils and Pots

Optimum growth happens when the right soil mix is used for the bonsai tree. The soil is among the most crucial factor for good growth and healthy development. Soils should provide adequate nutrient for the tree. Aside from this, soil should provide good aeration, drain water properly and adequately hold moisture.

Poor soil makes poor trees. Most often, bonsai that look unhealthy and lack vigor are often planted in poor soil. Incidentally, poor soil is often organic. The worst to use for bonsai are normal garden soil. It hardens easily when it dries, which does not help with growth. This can be disadvantageous for tree growth.

Factors to consider when mixing the right bonsai soil mix

Soil mixes specific for bonsai growing are available in garden shops and other similar establishments. But these may be a bit more costly than making a soil mix at home. Factors to take into consideration include the following:

Good water-retention

The soil mix should be able to retain just enough water to keep the soil moist and the tree well hydrated. It should hold too much water that can cause the roots to rot or to drown the tree.

Good drainage

Drainage is very important so that excess water can immediately flow out of the pot. If not, then it will soak the roots and cause them to rot. Excess water can also drown the bonsai tree. Also, soils that retain too much water do not have good aeration. Poor drainage also promotes the buildup of harmful salts.

Good aeration

Aeration refers to air flow in the soil. Tiny air pockets or gaps in between the soil particles are important to promote the better gas exchange. Nitrogen and carbon dioxide from the air should be able to flow into the soil to be absorbed by the roots or by the fungal and microbial community in the roots and soil. The mycorrhizae and good bacteria in the soil can live and process their food better when there is good air flow. This will allow them to produce more of the compounds that the roots can absorb. The absorbed compound are absorbed through the root hairs and brought to the leaves to be used as food.

Organic vs. Inorganic soil

Bonsai growing prefers using inorganic soils. This type of soil is particlebased, which allows for better control of aeration and drainage. When wellstructured, inorganic soils have good water drainage. The size of the particles allows food air circulation, fresh air continually flowing through the soil and among the roots to prevent rotting and promote healthy growth.

Organic soil tends to be compacted, or easily gets compacted as it settles in the pot. Compacted soils do not have any structure, which means lack of drainage and aeration. This will not support good root health, resulting in unhealthy tree development and rotting in the root system.

Despite the preference for inorganic soil, mixes still incorporate organic, as well as inorganic components. Organic soil mix includes bark, leaf litter, peat or other dead plant matter. Inorganic soil mix includes materials that have little or no organic compounds at al. Examples are fired clay, calcite or volcanic lava.

Recommended Soil Mixes for Bonsai

There are 3 basic soil mixes for bonsai growing. These are akadama, fine gravel (or grit) and organic potting compost.

Akadama is a type of Japanese clay that is hard-baked and specifically prepared for bonsai growing. It is always available for purchase in Bonsai shops. Before using, sift akadama. This will last for about 2 years and would have to be replaced once the particles start to break down. When akadama particles broke down, spaces for good aeration decrease. Akadama is somewhat expensive. To reduce the cost, baked or fired clay is often used as a substitute. These clays are available at any garden center, not necessarily in Bonsai shops. Cat litter may also be used as a substitute.

Grit or fine gravel

This is a very important component of soil mix for bonsai growing. It drains water and aerates the soil well. A layer of grit or fine gravel is placed at the bottom of the pot for better drainage.

Organic potting compost

Potting compost made with organic materials. This includes perlite, sand, and peat moss. Adding this component is important because this is where the vital nutrients needed for tree growth and development will come from. On their own, organic potting compost does not promote good drainage or aeration. It tends to hold too much water. Hence, it is a good balancing material for the other components that do not hold much water. Just make sure to limit how much is used to match the tree's needs and the grower's commitment to the bonsai's regular maintenance needs.

The type of soil mix depends on the tree species. In general, there are 2 types of soil mix used in bonsai tree growing. These are soil mix for coniferous tree species and for deciduous tree species. Both these basic mixes contain the 3 main soil mix components, namely, akadama, grit, and organic potting compost.

The following are general guidelines for mixing the soil. However, always take into consideration the climate where the tree is grown. Make adjustments accordingly. For example, more akadama and grit are added to the soil mix if the bonsai grows in a relatively wet climate.

Deciduous bonsai tree soil mix

    50% akadama

    25% grit

    25% organic potting compost

Coniferous bonsai tree (pine trees) soil mix

    60% akadama

    30% grit

10% organic potting compost

Guidelines for selecting the right bonsai pot

Japanese pottery is often the best pot to use for bonsai growing. These are high-quality pots, unglazed, natural and elegant but can be very expensive. Chinese pottery is often much cheaper compared to Japanese pottery. These generally are of lesser quality than Japanese ones but are currently improving to be considered as good pots or bonsai growing. Chinese pottery is commonly brightly glazed. An exception is Chinese antique pots. These antique pots are more expensive.

Old trees that have already been repotted for a number of times and already trained won't need frequent changes of pots compared to younger trees. Hence, more expensive pots can be used for these because they have already adapted well to life in small pots. For younger bonsai trees, repotting is more frequent, as the roots would need more room for growth. Training these would take a step-by-step process that involves a series of repotting. For this, it would be more economical to use plastic containers or less expensive pots.

Size

Size is another important consideration in choosing the right pot for bonsai trees. Trees that are still under training should be placed in larger containers. This will provide enough space for the roots to grow. Larger containers during the training period help the tree to cope better with the intensity of the training techniques applied to it, such as style-pruning. As the training progresses, the roots are gradually pruned until the tree has already adapted to growing in small pots. Once the trees have matured and are already trained, smaller pots can be used. The root systems should already be compact. At this point, aesthetic considerations are already among the prime reasons for bonsai pot choices.

Aesthetics

Aside from size, there are also other important considerations. These include shape, color and unglazed/glazed. To help with making the right choice, here are some guidelines. However, these are not hard and fast rules. Personal aesthetic choice will still play a larger role.

- Unglazed pots are commonly preferred among bonsai growers of pine trees and other conifers.

- Both unglazed and glazed bonsai pots can be used for deciduous trees. Experts recommend reserving the use of brightly glazed pots for trees that have flower and/or fruits.

- The width of the pot should approximately be equal to 2/3 of the bonsai tree's current height.

- How deep the pot is should be the same as the trunk base's thickness. However, this rule may be deferred when planting or repotting trees with very thin trunks or young bonsai trees.

- Angular pots are used for "masculine" type of trees. Rounded pots are used for "feminine" or gently shaped, slender bonsai trees.

And for all trees, the best, first and foremost guide to choosing pot is sturdiness. It should be large enough to support the tree's growth and sustain good health. Despite all the aesthetic choices, most bonsai experts prefer simplicity. The pot should enhance the natural beauty of the tree and not to compete with it. Its functionality should also always come first before aesthetics.

Application Of The Metal Wire

We now pass to another very important moment, that of the application of the metal wire, which is essential for the tree to grow according to the desired shape.

Pruning is a very important part of shaping your bonsai, but if you want to truly shape your bonsai into the shape you desire, then you will need to take it a step further and wire your bonsai. By wrapping wire around the trunk and branches of your bonsai, you are able to manipulate exactly where and how you want the branches to grow. When the tree is flexible, it's easy to move the bonsai into the position that you would like, but it's rather complicated to keep it there. Having the sturdiness of the wire allows for the tree to be molded and then remain in the position it was placed in. It will take a few months, but as soon as the branches are set, the wire can be removed. The bonsai will continue to grow in the style that it was adjusted into.

Bonsais can be wired at any time of year and it can be performed at your own preference. The only species of trees that should be wired in winter are deciduous trees and any other trees that lose their leaves in colder temperatures. The reason for this is because it's much easier to wire the bonsais when your vision isn't obstructed by foliage. But it is important to pay attention during this time because even though the nutrients in foliage don't go to the foliage, large branches can grow thicker in the winter months and, if this occurs, it can create scarring if the wires start digging into the flesh of the branches.

If you notice that the branches are growing at an accelerated rate, remove the wiring around the bonsai and replace it at a later stage. Scarring from wires that have broken the bark of a bonsai will most likely be permanent, so it should be avoided as best as possible.

Types Of Wires

There are two types of wires that can be considered when wiring bonsais:

Suitable wires are copper or aluminum and for some types of trees, such as maple, apricot and thorns, it is convenient to use plastic-coated threads or wrapped in paper.

Neither one of these wires rust and both have a strong tensile strength. Aluminum wire is better for use in deciduous bonsais, while copper wire is better for use in pine and conifer trees. That being said, the aluminum wire does work well with practically all species of bonsais and is the easiest to use as a beginner enthusiast.

The diameter will be of different sizes depending on the thickness and strength of the branch to be corrected.

Usually, a wire 1/3 of the diameter of the branch or trunk to be wrapped is used.

Wires come in a variety of thicknesses (1 - 8 mm) but the best ones for beginners don't exceed 4 mm in thickness. The thicker wires should be used on the larger branches and you can use thinner wires as you move up and along the bonsai. It is best to first wrap the trunk and thick branches in palm fiber (raffia) that has been soaked in water. This prevents scarring on the thicker sections of the bonsai. If thinner branches are scarred, they can always be removed, but this isn't a possibility with the trunk and main branches. So extra precautions are necessary.

How To Wire Your Bonsai

Wiring your bonsai is going to be very tricky and you are going to make mistakes. But as you have learned to be more patient with the entire growing process of your bonsai, you will get the technique right when you practice it. While you are still starting out, consider double-wiring certain branches that are close together because wrapping them together allows support for the branches and allows slightly more space for you to work.

Before proceeding with the application, it is advisable to fix the wire to the ground or to the trunk, always starting from the backside, so as to hide the origin of the binding or not to leave too much play.

Especially for the first case, in fact, it would damage the bark of the tree, risking the wire embedding itself in the bonsai. In this case, it is better to cut the metal wire and leave the part embedded in the shaft, to avoid even greater injuries.

The wire should be wound at an angle of 45 degrees to the trunk or branch, avoiding tying both leaves and buds.

The period of time in which to maintain the binding is different depending on the style chosen and the type of tree: Indicatively, it varies from 6-8 months of deciduous plants to 18 months of conifers.

The thread will preferably be removed in the autumn before the vegetative stasis. It is good to remember not to apply during the vegetative awakening of the plant, not to practice it on newly repotted or repotted bonsai trees, as each of these operations considerably weakens the plant.

Once the wire has been applied, the plant will be kept in a place sheltered from the sun and wind, spraying and watering often.

The metal wire is the main technique for changing the shape of the plant; however, there are other ways to correct it.

Once you have got the hang of this method, use single-wiring on the branches that can't be double-wired. Don't shape the branches until you have wrapped the entire tree because if you start shaping it too early you may get confused with what to do with the remainder of the branches if you designed your desired style. Waiting until the end to shape allows you to move everything more smoothly and sequentially.

When wiring an entire bonsai, start at the bottom of the trunk and then move up to the primary branches. Once those are done, use a thinner wire to wrap the secondary branches and up into the foliage. As a general rule, use a wire that is ⅓ as thick as the branch that you are wiring. That thickness will allow for enough structural support to style the bonsai.

After you have completed the entire process of wiring the bonsai (which will take a long time, so be patient), you can start to form it into the shape you desire. Grip the branches firmly with your thumb and index finger and start bending them slowly. Even though the branches are flexible, they can still break, so move slowly and gently. Once the branch is positioned, do not move it again.

Once your bonsai has been styled according to your specifications, move it outside and into a shady spot if it's in the warmer months. Fertilize your bonsai as you normally would and keep a close eye on it because you don't want the tree to grow and get scarred. When you remove the wiring, you need to cut the wires at every turn and not unwind it.

Unwinding the wiring almost always damages the bark on the bonsai and it will leave avoidable scarring.

In fact, you can also use cords attached to the container, to another support, or to the trunk itself to keep the branches in tension.

Other times stones or weights can be tied to a branch in order to change its direction of development.

Finally, with small wooden dowels, it is possible to spread two branches considered too close.

Of all these techniques, however, that of the metal wire is the most used, as it allows a more precise action on the branches and on the trunk.

Shaping the Trunk

Aside from the roots, the trunk is another fundamental aspect of the bonsai tree. This is the most attractive part and captures the very essence of nature. The appearance of the trunk also creates the illusion of age. It is the central attraction of any bonsai. Its shape also influences where the branches will be located, how much the leaves will be reduced, distribution of foliage, etc.

The first step in shaping the trunk is to develop it into a well-formed one. Factors to add after shaping the trunk include developing a good taper, called *kokejun*. It is also important to give good support the trunk's initial rise, called the *tachiagari*. Smooth curves and other aesthetic preferences can be initiated, too.

When working with a tree that has already reached bonsai stage, even if still in the early parts, consider how to best present charm and grace into the shape of the tree. Pay attention to the trunk's shape. This will determine what traditional bonsai tree forms will be followed.

Once a form has been decided, focus on the how to display the tree's tape or *kokejun*, which embodies a giant tree, the initial rise or *tachiagari*, or the smooth curves of the tree.

Displaying the *kokejun*

Trees growing naturally in the ground have thick, large trunks at the base. As the trunk extends upwards, it gradually becomes narrow. This is what the taper or *kokejun* refers to. However, not all trees suitable for bonsai growing have this taper. To achieve the natural tree taper as found in nature, it has to be made. The trunk has to be shaped this way.

For a good *kokejun* to develop, develop a larger initial rise or *tachiagari* by promoting branch growth. Once the *tachiagari* developed into the desired thickness, trim off the branches. This will form a good *kokejun*. At this point, provide adequate water and nutrition to the tree because more of these will promote thicker trunk growth. Also, more branches would help in increasing the flow of water and nutrition. Every time some of the branches are cut off, the flow of water and nutrients decrease. The trunk will narrow in this condition. The trunk's thickness is directly related to how much water and nutrients flow through it. Trees tend to have more flow of nutrients and water in the top parts. To promote more flow and thickening of the lower portion, prune some of the top leaves and branches. Continue doing this and with a good amount of fertilizer and sunlight exposure, the *kokejun* will eventually form sufficiently in a few years.

Buds growing from stumps can help thicken the trunk of trees like Chinese elm. Wait 2 months after the appearance of new buds in the early summer before bending the tree and securing it with wires. This will form the desired shape of the tree. After 4 months, in the late autumn, prune the tree again. Wires for shaping the trees should only be used while the tree is young. Repeat this in the 2nd and 3rd year to reinforce the shape. Over the years, the trunk will thicken and enlarge.

Tatekae

The *tatekae* technique is another method for creating and developing the *kokejun*. This technique means trunk reshaping by cutting back. This technique can be used both on the trunk or any of the branches. The branch needed to make the taper is identified. The trunk above the chosen branch is cut off. The remaining branch is then allowed and nurtured to grow into the new trunk. This method is often preferred in developing the *kokejun* because the branch is thinner than the tree trunk, making it more pliable and easier to shape into the desired appearance.

If this branch grows and almost upturns, it forms the *chokkan* or the formal upright form. Adjust the growing direction of this branch and it will develop into a trunk in the *moyoghi* or informal upright form.

While it is easier to shape the trunk into the desired shape and form, this will take a longer time before the *kokejun* appears natural. The scars created by cutting off the trunk and/or branches will take time to heal and become almost inconspicuous.

This method can cause some tree species to become more prone to withering.

For these species, pay closer attention to when and how much to prune. Fertilizing before and after the trunk or branches are also pruned helps to prevent withering and promotes larger trunk size.

Displaying the tachiagari

The *tachiagari* is the part where the tree's main characteristic is prominently displayed. This main feature is found at the *ichi-no-eda* portion, which is the tree shape found in between the first branch and the roots. This is also what the "initial rise" refers to- the point where the trunk initially rises from the ground.

The initial rise or *tachiagari* differs among the different bonsai forms. In the *chokkan* or formal upright form, the *tachiagari* is energetically growing straight and upwards. In the *moyohai*, the initial rise of the trunk is displayed in a way that showcases the smooth curves. In the *bunjingi* bonsai style, the initial rise highlights the elegant and gentle smoothness of the tree trunk.

The *tachegiri* is meant to highlight the trunk's natural beauty and characteristics. Special attention is given to the portion between the roots to the first naturally growing branch (*ichi-no-da*), then between the 1st branch to the 2nd branch (*ni-no-eda*) and from the 2nd branch to the 3rd branch (*san-noeda*). The location of these 1st 3 branches, angles at which they grow from the trunk, length and relation to the trunk and the rest of the tree have major impacts on the beauty of the bonsai tree. These 3 are key to achieving and fully realizing the aesthetics of the bonsai.

The *tachiagari* can be created by following the process of creating the *kokejun*. In case the tree has already gone past a certain stage, for instance, the *ichi-no-eda* has already grown too long, air layering can be done to shorten it.

Plant Diseases

We now begin a very important chapter in the care of bonsai, as it can often happen that a plant shows symptoms of a disease that is difficult to recognize and, therefore, to cure. In fact, due to its size, the bonsai is more defenseless than the normal plants against the attacks of many adversities, therefore it is the bonsai artist's job to quickly recognize the diseases and help his plant.

When the bonsai begins to weaken, it is immediately necessary to check whether there are deficiencies or excesses of some kind in its care and maintenance: In what position is the plant about to the wind and light? At what level are humidity and temperature? Is it fed in the right way? All these factors must always be kept under control, but sometimes the bad health of our bonsai can derive from other causes.

Bonsai trees, like most other plants on earth, are susceptible to parasites, fungi, and insects that can greatly damage them. Since there are so many things that can attack your bonsai, the best case of treatment, in this case, is prevention. If you keep your tree healthy, it will be able to fight off many infections and fungi without much external help, because many trees can mount their own defenses against these attacks.

If you balance your water, fertilizer, and light requirements for your bonsai, it will most likely stay healthy and continue to grow for years. But one of the worst problems that enthusiasts make is to put their bonsai in the wrong location. If the tree doesn't have good lighting and good air circulation, it will be more susceptible to developing a problem.

Additionally, it is necessary that you keep the area around your bonsai as hygienic as possible. If you take the effort of cleaning the area where your bonsais are situated, there is a greatly reduced risk of your tree(s) developing problems, but sometimes there are problems that can arise that even healthy trees can't ward off — pests.

Animal And Plant Pests

It is important to bear in mind that bonsai are subject to the same pests and diseases as the species of the trees to which they belong. Therefore, in principle, as regards diseases due to plant or animal parasites, a bonsai, if in full force, has the potential to defend itself.

A constant cure would, therefore, be sufficient to prevent and avoid diseases of this type.

However, this does not exclude that, during the weakening phases due to repotting or pruning, the bonsai can get sick.

Among the animal parasites, we find various types of insects that damage the plant by using it for their nourishment.

The most common are:

- Ants

Description: Ants on your bonsai are a dangerous sign because ants and aphids normally work together. The reason for this is because ants and aphids have a co-dependent relationship where the ants carry the eggs of aphids to suitable vegetation because the aphids will eventually produce a sweet, sugary substance known as "honeydew" which the ants thrive on. The ants aren't really a problem on your bonsai, but their little passengers are definitely something to worry about.

Ants may not be a problem themselves, but the problems that they carry with them can be severely devastating to your bonsai. Ants don't only carry aphid eggs, but they can also carry a black sooty fungus that starts to destroy the bark of trees. Additionally, ants are known to make their nests in bonsai pots and can disrupt the root system of your bonsai.

*Symptoms:*If you notice that ants are starting to nest in your bonsai's pot, then it indicates that you aren't watering your tree correctly. But, in the cases of trees like pines, which prefer drier soil, sometimes this can't be changed because adding additional water could hurt your tree.

Cure: In cases like these, it's better to use a gentle pesticide that won't hurt the roots of your tree. Pesticides like Bungy, Kemprin, and Koinor are your best options for treating problems at a root level.

- Anthracnose

Description: Anthracnose is an umbrella term that includes several fungal infections that affect trees. These fungi thrive on plant material where it inoculates and then spreads very quickly. If a bonsai is kept in a warm, humid, shady place, these fungi will spread like wildfire and damage your bonsai.

Unfortunately, during the warmth of the growing seasons along with young foliage starting to develop, anthracnose is a serious risk and you need to keep a close eye on any signs of it developing. When leaves become thicker and more leathery, they are far more resilient to fungal infections, but young leaves are very susceptible.

Symptoms: The symptoms of these types of infections are very easy to spot, but they still seem to go unnoticed by enthusiasts who don't know what they're looking for. One of the indicative symptoms is the drying and curling of leaves that look like they've been burned. As the fungal infection worsens, more and more brown spots will spread to more leaves and will continuously look like the tree is being scorched even though it may be in a shady spot.

Not all trees are susceptible to these types of infections and they are practically unheard of in species like conifers and evergreens. Deciduous trees, on the other hand, have much softer leaves and seem to be far more susceptible to these types of infections

Even though these types of infections are rather unsightly on your bonsai, they aren't normally severe enough to kill the tree. They usually only cause the death of one or two branches at a time, but if left untreated, it can eventually spread into the trunk of the tree and that can lead to its death.

Cure: If you notice that your bonsai is infected with this type of infection, it will spread to your other trees and plants if you aren't careful. It is important to quarantine any bonsais with these possible infections and keep them away from other plants. Just like human infections, these types of infections can spread very easily to any other plants close to them so quarantining them is one of the best actions.

Once that is done, spray your tree with chemical sprays designed to treat anthracnose infections and repeat the treatment until it starts working. It is also necessary to remove all of the infected leaves and branches as far as possible and spray the rest of the tree down on a daily basis. Keep the tree in a highly lit area and watch the bonsai closely for any brown spots on the uninfected leaves.

- Aphids

Description: Even though an infestation of ants is normally indicative of an aphid infestation, aphids are also known to attack plants by themselves. Aphids are one of the most common and one of the most detrimental pests to bonsais. Aphids burrow into the soft areas of plants and start sucking out the sap. But this has a dual problem because the plant is losing a lot of its nutrients and aphids regularly carry diseases that attack plants from the inside.

Any little bugs that appear to be green, black, or gray are most likely aphids and if you spot them, they should be treated quickly. Aphids attack plants and manage to devour large sections of the plants in a very small amount of time, so it's important to check under your bonsai's leaves on a regular basis to keep any problems from arising.

Symptoms: If you notice that the leaves and branches on your bonsai seem to be weaker than normal, it could be indicative of an aphid attack. Additionally, if you notice that new leaves that are sprouting seem to be curled and unhealthy, then your suspicions may be confirmed. The reason why the new growth comes out looking like that is that the nutrients are so leached out by the aphids that the tree can't adequately support new growth.

Cure: If this is a problem that is affecting your bonsai, then you will need to wash the leaves with a stream of water. But ensure that you don't harm the tree further. Additionally, there are some gentle baby shampoos that can be used. Make a diluted solution and wash the leaves. The aphids can't breathe with the soap covering them and they either leave or die. A few repetitions of this should clear up the infestation.

You can consider other insecticides or you can move your bonsai to an area that has a high population of ladybugs. Ladybugs are carnivorous little beetles and they devour aphids without harming your bonsai. There are many insects that you want in your garden and ladybugs are definitely one of them!

- Borer

Description: Tree borers consist of different species of insects that lay their eggs on or underneath a tree's bark. When the eggs hatch and the larvae start to squirm out, they immediately look for sustenance and they start to burrow deeper into the tree, eating the woody flesh as they move deeper.

As the larvae grow, their appetites will also increase, and because they may be burrowing into the trunk of your bonsai, there may be serious problems that will develop soon after they get deeper into the lumen.

Symptoms: It is possible to miss the adult insects on your bonsai, but you will notice the signs that larvae have started to burrow into your bonsai. There will be signs of holes and even sawdust around the base of the tree.

Cure: This type of infestation is definitely one of the most difficult to treat and if the larvae have made it into the trunk, it might be untreatable. There are pesticides that you can try, but the real problem is that the death of the wood is going to affect your bonsai's aesthetics forever. If you have other bonsai, it might be best to get rid of the infected bonsai to prevent it from spreading to any of your other trees.

It may be a difficult decision, but it may be the most prudent in cases like these.

- Caterpillars

Description: Caterpillars are the larvae stage of butterflies and moths and even though most of their damage is caused above ground, they do have voracious appetites.

Symptoms: Caterpillars of all sixes can consume large quantities of leaves in a very small space of time.

Fortunately, it's very easy to see if caterpillars have attacked your bonsai and you will be able to take action quickly.

Cure: The best treatment, in this case, is to actually remove them by hand. This may be time-consuming, and some caterpillars are small and camouflaged, but it is better for your bonsai and the environment if you are able to avoid using pesticides. It is also useful to make a solution of baby shampoo and rub it on the leaves of your bonsai. If there is a form of soap on the leaves, the caterpillars won't want to eat them.

- Mealybugs

Description: Mealybugs are white, furry insects that produce a waxy covering to protect themselves from the elements and from larger predators. These types of insects are found underneath leaves and sometimes in the root systems of plants. So, when you are repotting your bonsai, it's always necessary to check the roots for any indications of these little creatures.

Symptoms: Just like aphids, mealybugs burrow in and start sucking the sap of the tree or plant. Leaves will start to droop and look unhealthy. They will move from vibrant green to a more yellow discoloration until the leaf dies. If left untreated, the tree will take strain because of the lack of nutrients so it does need to be addressed quickly.

Cure: Using an acidic solution of lime or lemon juice in these cases helps for the treatment of mealy bugs and the acid can effectively kill them. If this isn't successful you can increase the treatment to a pesticide that is safe to use on trees.

- Red Spider Mites

Description: Red spider mites are a tiny pest and even though they are smaller than aphids, they are much faster moving and can kill a plant at an accelerated rate. Once red spider mites settle on a tree, they get to work very quickly.

The main problem with these types of mites is their size. Because they're so small they are very easy to overlook and not notice. Only if one is very close to the leaves can they see the little mites moving and even then, it's when one knows what they're looking for.

Symptoms: The first indication that enthusiasts normally see that there's a problem is that the leaves on their bonsais start to get yellow and brown blotches on the leaves of their bonsai.

Cure: The treatment for these types of mites is normally with a pesticide because they spread so rapidly. It is best to quarantine your bonsai to prevent further spread and then treat as best as you can. If you catch the infection early and treat the mites rapidly, your bonsai should recover to its full health.

● *White Grubs*

Description: Most pests target the top of the trees but grubs, on the other hand, go straight for the root systems of trees and larger plants. This means that the root systems of bonsais are susceptible to the larvae of several different beetles known as grubs. And, unfortunately, there is no way of knowing there is a problem until the problems start to manifest themselves above ground.

Symptoms: Because grubs attack the roots, the tree will seem healthy at first, but it will start to seem more sickly over time. Pay attention to the leaves of your bonsai and if you notice that the leaves are starting to wilt regardless of what you do, and if you can't see any other problems on the surface, then the problem may be lying underground. There may be some evidence of adult beetle attacks on your bonsai if the leaves have been eaten. You can differentiate a beetle's bite marks from those of caterpillars or snails by the fact that beetle's eat notches into leaves instead of in circular patterns. The indicative U-shape holes are normally created by beetles.

Cure: If your bonsai is looking unhealthy and there is evidence of this, it's best to remove the tree from its pot and inspect the roots. It will be easy to spot any grubs in the root system and they can easily be removed by hand.

• *Scale*

Description: Scale pests are insects that come in a variety of shapes, sizes, and colors. These insects range from white to yellow to black and even though they move around a lot when they're younger, they tend to find one place that they're comfortable in when they're nearing adulthood and then hunker down and dig into the flesh of the plant they are on.

Once they have burrowed through the protective layers of the plant, they start to drink the sap, but unlike other insects, these stay put and don't move once they have found their spot.

Symptoms: Because they take up permanent residence on one site and have a shiny covering, they resemble scales.

Cure: The best treatment for these types of infections is to physically remove them by hand. Because the insects don't move, they are easy to scrape off with your fingernails and then rinse off. Once you have removed all of the scales it's advisable to apply some bonsai cut cream to the areas to prevent infection.

- Snails and Slugs

Description: Everyone has probably seen slugs and snails in the gardens at some point or another and these pests can be very destructive to plant life. They thrive in damp conditions and are most common during the warm, rainy seasons.

Symptoms: Even though they are very slow-moving, they are able to strip an entire bonsai of its leaves in a matter of hours.

Cure: The best treatment against these pests is to go out at night with a flashlight and search for them. Because they are mostly nocturnal, they are very active at night and they like to move around more in cooler temperatures, so they will come out of hiding. If you suspect that there may be a problem in your garden or around your bonsais, then a bit of nocturnal hunting may do the trick to protect your bonsais.

- Laniger aphid and white cochineal

Description: They are small insects that develop at the expense of the plant, surrounding themselves with a white waxy substance and feeding on the sap.

Symptoms: White and woolly formations wrap around the petioles of the leaves and the divergence of the branches, weakening the plant.

Cure: Use Croneton or Compron on the soil, or water with Ekamet or Proposcur at 0.15%.

- Black aphid

Description: It is an insect that lives in colonies, spreading especially in spring and creating blackish formations attached to sheets and flowers. This slows down the development of the plant in the affected areas.

Symptoms: Dark windings hit the shoots and stretch to the leaves and flowers.

Cure: Use Croneton and Primor without affecting the flowers.

- Cochineal

Description: It is an insect that feeds on the sap of plants, injecting a chemical substance inside that causes an abundant secretion of sugars. *Symptoms:* In the lower part of the leaves dark-colored folds are created.

Care: It would sometimes be sufficient to remove the animals from the plant with a simple stick, however, the use of Primor or 0.2% Aphisan, sprayed on the plant, or Croneton poured into the ground is recommended.

- ***Phylloxeraradicicol***

Description: It is a female aphid of small size, green or yellow-brown, which lays a large number of eggs and attacks the roots of plants.

Symptoms: The plant tends to turn yellow and deteriorate. Looking at the roots or the earth, one can notice small gray-white ball formations.

Cure: Pour on the ground of Croneton or a solution of Metasystox or Alphos.

- Whitefly or Aleuroids

Description: The whitefly is a white insect whose larvae, hidden under the leaves, feed on the sap of the plant, forcing it to emit various sugary productions. It mainly affects plants such as Lantana and Segerezia. ***Symptoms:*** The leaves begin to turn yellow at the bottom and weaken.

Care: The use of products such as Folithion, Ambush, or Undene is recommended.

- Lice or aphids

Description: Lice and aphids are insects that live in rather large groups, attaching themselves to the trunk and leaves to suck the sap. Some species are equipped with wings and, moving from plant to plant, they also favor the spread of viruses. *Symptoms:* Insect groups cover leaves and buds that weaken and decay.

Cure: There may be enough water to remove them. Otherwise use Primor or Croneton, or spray with Parexan or another spray.

- Red spider or garden mite

Description: They are small red, yellow or brown spiders that make their nests on the leaves on the branches. They attack both fruit trees and plants of other species.

Symptoms: The leaves are wrapped in very thin cobwebs on which it is possible to notice animals with a lens. Over time the leaves turn yellow and weaken.

Cure: We recommend using Tetagril on the ground, or spraying the plant with special Lizetan or Metasystox R, particularly suitable against these insects.

Plant parasites are caused by conditions of the particular weakness of the plant that facilitate the spread of diseases.

- *Chlorosis*

Description: It is a disease due to a lack of iron or excess calcium in the soil. Factors that prevent easy absorption of mineral substances cause a serious deficiency of chlorophyll inside the plant.

Symptoms: The leaves begin to turn yellow, but leave the ribs green, and wither.

Cure: Before watering, pour Fetrilon or Sequestrene into the right amount.

- ### Sooty mold

Description: They are fungi that affect the bonsai in the trunk, in the leaves and the branches, giving rise to dark incrustations. Mushrooms often feed on sugary substances caused by the passage of aphids and above all are favored by high humidity and poor ventilation.

Symptoms: Dark-colored spots or sooty areas are created in the affected areas.

Cure: We recommend the use of Cupravit or Baymat, or in any case of any product with copper oxychloride.

- Radical rot

Description - Symptoms: The best treatment for this problem is prevention. It is best to not overwater your bonsai and also keep the ground in the pot clear of any fallen foliage. Sometimes, infected leaves can drop onto the soil and infect it with a fungus, so it's best to remove them when you notice some leaves have died and fallen off. It is also necessary to ensure that your tree is an area that is well-ventilated and has decent exposure to sunlight.

If you suspect that your bonsai may have root rot, it is best to remove your bonsai from its pot and prune away all of the infected roots. This may or not work because of the severity of the fungal spread, but it is worth the try. Once all of the infected roots have been pruned, the tree needs to be planted in fastdraining soil.

The roots rot mainly for two reasons: Excessive fertilization, which causes damage and necrosis, and an excessively abundant watering, which causes water to stagnate in the soil.

Root rot is a problem that all bonsais face because they spend their lives in pots. This problem is caused by a fungus because of poor drainage in the pot. Plants and trees that are planted in the ground don't usually face this problem but it is a risk for any potted tree or plant.

As soon as the water starts to back up and the roots sit in unnecessary fluid, they become much softer and at risk for fungal infections. If roots turn brown and take on a mushy-like consistency, the tree won't be able to draw up water and nutrients any longer and the tree will inevitably die.

It is important to note that not all fungi in roots are bad things and root rot shouldn't be confused with the white fungus that grows in the roots of pine trees because that fungus is absolutely essential to the pine trees' survival.

The plant weakens and begins to perish, due to the Tadice's inability to forfeit nourishment, the leaves take on a dark color.

Cure:

Severe root rot can be treated with Lime Sulfur, a broad-acting fungicide, and it may be able to kill the fungus. If there are roots still strong enough to heal, there still may be a chance of survival. But it's definitely best not to let it get to this point and rather prevent it from occurring altogether.

It is good to cut the sick and already dead roots and leave the healthy ones in a solution of Benomyl or Orthocid, after having cleaned them well from the ground.

Kiplantate the bonsai in a pot with new soil, keeping the soil watered and moist fertilizing should be practiced only after 2 months.

- ***Powdery mildew or Spaerotheca***

Description: They are also fungi that affect the plant in particular conditions of temperature and ventilation. Their propagation is facilitated by the particular heat and humidity, so it is good to be particularly careful in the summer.

Symptoms: Powdery mildew creates a whitish powder-like substance on the front of the leaves and in the other affected points, gradually weakening the plant.

Cure: To eliminate powdery mildew in a short time, you can use any fungicide or even a KB solution of micronized sulfur to be administered every 15 days.

- False powdery mildew

Description: It is a mushroom similar to the previous one, even if it manifests itself differently way. It is favored by inadequate conditions of temperature and humidity.

Symptoms: It determines a gray moldy substance in the lower part of the leaves, while it turns yellow the upper one, staining some points of gray.

Cure: Use Bayleton or CupravitBlu, spraying it in the relevant points, transporting the bonsai to a well-ventilated place

- ***Virosis***

Description: These are all the diseases caused by the spread of viruses which, however, are still not easily identifiable today and which often occur in a deleterious way for plants.

The virus spreads easily or through insects, or due to infected tools, or in any circumstance in which some wounds of the tree can be affected, such as in the case of grafts, pruning, etc.

Symptoms: The symptoms are various and are not always recognizable in a short time. In the most common cases, these are streaks of various colors that are highlighted on the leaves;

regardless of the symptoms the fate of the plant is however probably sealed.

Cure: Unfortunately, there are few remedies after a plant has been affected.

You can only try to make sure that the infection does not expand, moving the plant away. Above all, however, it is recommended to prevent virosis by fighting animal parasites and keeping tools clean.

22 Plants Datasheets

We now give a list of the main characteristics of each type of bonsai plant, indispensable for taking care of all the processing phases.

In case you are interested in a bonsai whose name is not in the list, know that the indications you find for a certain species can also be applied to any other plant in the same family.

ARALIA MING (POLYSCIAS FRUCTICOSA)

Family: Araliaceae

Description: Aralia Ming is a large shrub from Polynesia and tropical Asia. It is characterized by a wrinkled golden-green trunk, dense branches and tender leaves, supported by a very elongated petiole.

Environment and exposure: It can be kept next to a very bright window, even exposed to direct sunlight, if these are not too strong. In summer it can be taken out in a sunny place, while in winter it prefers an environment with temperatures between 18 and 20 degrees Celsius- 64.4-68 F..

Watering: The Aralia Ming must be kept always humid, with continuous watering and spraying often also on the leaves.

Fertilization: It is recommended to fertilize from March to September with liquid fertilizer, every 2 weeks. In the winter stasis, on the other hand, you only have to fertilize once every 4-5 weeks.

Repotting: It is good to repot at least once every two during the beginning of spring, to shorten and cut the roots.

Soil: The ideal soil consists of a mixture of clay for 1/4, of peat for 2/4, and of sand for the remaining 1/4.

Pruning: The branches can always be sprouted or cut throughout the year the shoots instead they are topped in groups of 2-3 pairs when they have reached 5-6 pairs. It is also good to eliminate too large leaves.

Binding: The Aralia Ming has a structure that is not suitable for binding, both because of the shape it naturally assumes and because the practice is not very effective.

Multiplication: Multiplication with the cutting method is recommended.

AZALEA (AZALEA INDICA)

Family: Ericaceae

Description: It is a subtropical shrub from East Asia, characterized by colorful flowers and bright green leaves.

Flowering: In the period from spring to autumn, flowers bloom can be white, pink, red, orange, or purple.

Environment and exposure: All year round it can be kept near a bright and ventilated window. In summer you can take it out without ever exposing it to the sun. In winter it prefers temperatures between 5 and 10 degrees Celsius – 41-50 F..

Watering: For the summer period it is good to water continuously and in abundance. In winter it is sufficient to keep the soil quite humid.

Fertilization: It can be fertilized only in summer, with liquid fertilizer, administered once every 2 weeks, completely stopping for the winter.

Repotting: It is necessary to repot once every 2-3 years, after flowering, cutting and sprouting too long roots.

Soil: The most suitable mixture for Azalea consists of clay for 1/5, peat for 2/5 and sand for the other 2/5.

Pruning: Branches can always be cut; on the contrary, the shoots are topped to decrease the number of leaves from 6 pairs to 2-3 pairs. Also, wilted flowers must be eliminated to allow the plant to develop seeds.

Binding: It is possible to practice it on branches and shoots that are sufficiently lignified, however particular attention is necessary due to the fragile structure of the plant.

Multiplication: The most suitable is the multiplication by cutting.

BAMBOO (BAMBUSA HUMILIS)

Family: Araminaceae

Description: It is a plant native to China and India, characterized by a hollow, gnarled and elongated stem. The leaves are pointed and light green in color.

Environment and exposure: All year round it can be housed near a bright window, although it is recommended to take it outside in the summer, without placing it in the sun. For winter the ideal temperature is between 15 and 18 degrees Celsius – 59-64 F..

Watering: Watering must be regular and abundant throughout the year to keep the soil constantly humid.

Fertilization: Fertilization is recommended only in the period from March to September, using liquid fertilizer, once every 2 weeks.

Repotting: Repotting always in spring every one or two years, depending on the age of the plant, by shortening and cutting the roots.

Soil: The ideal mixture consists of 2/5 of clay, 2/5 of sand, and 1/5 of peat.

Pruning: It is recommended to carefully trim the shoots, to reduce the size of the bonsai.

Binding: The structure of the Bamboo makes the application of the metal wire inadvisable.

Multiplication: Among the various methods, the one that obtains the best results is the multiplication by cutting.

BEECH (FAGUS SYLVATICA)

Family: fagaceae

Description: large tree native to areas of southern Europe and western Asia. It is characterized by a gray and smooth trunk, by thin and abundant branches and by bright green oval leaves.

Environment and exposure: Beech should be kept in a very bright area, near a sunny window. In summer it can be taken outside, in the half-light, or the sun if this is not too strong. In winter, winter, the temperature must be between 12 and 15 degrees Celsius - 53-59 F

Watering: it is advisable to water abundantly and regularly throughout the year, preventing the soil from drying out.

Fertilization: for the whole period from March to October, it is necessary to fertilize once every 3 weeks. In the winter period instead, it is sufficient to give fertilizer every 4 or 5 weeks.

Repotting: repotting should be practiced once every year, during the beginning of spring, by cutting and shortening too long roots.

Soil: the most suitable mixture for beech, is made up of clay, peat and cage in equal proportions

Pruning: the branches can be pruned in spring and early autumn. The shoots are topped to decrease the number of leaves from 5-6 pairs to 2-3.

Binding: it is important to remember that as regards the Beech it is preferable to practice the binding after the shoots are cut, on well-lignified branches and twigs.

Multiplication: methods by seed and by cuttings are recommended.

BIRCH (BETULA NIGRA)

Family: Betulaceae

__Description:__ Shrub native to cold temperate regions, characterized by the stem and thin branches and by pointed and serrated leaves.

__Environment and exposure:__ Birch must be kept in a very bright and ventilated place. For the summer period, it is recommended to take it outside without exposing it too much to the sun. In winter it is better to maintain a temperature between 10 and 15 degrees Celsius – 50-59 F..

__Watering:__ Throughout the period between April and October it is advisable to water regularly, keeping the soil constantly humid. In winter it is possible to decrease the doses of water while preventing the soil from drying out too much.

__Fertilization:__ Fertilization should be practiced only in the period between May and September, distributing fertilizer, preferably liquid, once every 3 weeks.

__Repotting:__ The most suitable time for repotting is once every two years, at the beginning of spring, just before the buds appear.

__Soil:__ The most suitable mixture to meet the needs of birch must be rather acidic, therefore we recommend a mixture of 1/4 of clay, 2/4 of peat, and 1/4 of sand.

Pruning: It is better to prune the branches in the period just before the growth of the shoots; even if the operation guarantees good results throughout the year. The shoots should be sprouted from 5-6 pairs of leaves to 1-2 pairs.

Binding: Summer is the most suitable time to apply metal wire. It should be remembered, however, to pay particular attention to the degree of robustness of the branches and shoots.

Multiplication: Birch can be multiplied by seed and cutting methods.

BOX-TREE (BUXUS HARLANDII)

Family: Buxaceae

Description: Boxtree is an evergreen shrub characteristic of the Far East and Mediterranean coasts. The thick foliage and the abundance of branches have highlighted it as an excellent plant for hedges. Its branches are often cut in a particular way to obtain geometric shapes or other types of figures.

Flowering: Small flowers develop in the winter period from November to January.

Environment and exposure: The box-tree needs a bright and cool place so we recommend placing it near a window throughout the year. If in summer you want to take it outside, from May to September, it is good to leave it in a place protected from direct sun. In winter it is good to keep the temperature between 10 and 15 degrees Celsius – 50-59 F..

Watering: Watering must be very abundant in summer and repeated every time the soil dries. In winter, it is best to decrease the intensity to a few times a week, depending on the needs of the plant.

Fertilization: Fertilization must be practiced for the whole period from spring to autumn. We recommend a liquid fertilizer for bonsai, every twenty days or so. If the bonsai is placed in a warm place even in winter, it can be fertilized once every 35-40 days.

Repotting: It is recommended to practice it every two years, at the arrival of spring, cutting and shortening all the roots.

Soil: It is recommended to make a mixture of 2/5 of the earth for bonsai or clay, 2/5 of sand, and 1/5 of peat.

Pruning: The branches can be pruned throughout the year. When clusters of leaves are born, it is recommended that the number be reduced to two or three pairs.

Binding: Possible throughout the year.

Multiplication: We recommend using the cutting method.

BUGANVILLEA (BOUGAINVILLEA GLABRA)

Family: nictaginaceae

Description: it is a shrub from the areas of Brazil and southern America, characterized by long, thorny branches and smooth, light green-green leaves.

Flowering: in the period from June to September it develops small flowers covered with bracts with very bright colors.

__Environment and exposure:__ all year round it can be positioned next to a window in an illuminated and ventilated area. In the period from May to September, it can also be placed outside in a sunny position. In winter we recommend a temperature between 10 and 15 degrees Celsius – 50-59 F.

__Watering:__ for the summer period, the soil must be watered regularly to keep it moist, but in moderation so as not to risk dropping the leaves. For the winter, the soil will be left completely dry before supplying new water.

__Fertilizing:__ especially in the fertilization period: yes, in summer, by administering fertilizer every 15-20 days. In winter we will limit ourselves to fertilizing once every 4-5 weeks.

Repotting: repotting should be practiced once every 2 or 3 years, at the arrival of spring, by cutting and sprouting the overdeveloped roots.

__Soil:__ the most suitable mixture consists of 2/5 of clay, 2/5 of peat and 1/5 of sand.

__Pruning:__ we recommend pruning the branches and shoots all year round, except during the flowering period.

Multiplication: the most suitable method is that of cutting, to be practiced in spring.

CAMELLIA JAPONICA (CAMELIA JAPONICA)

Family: Theaceae

Description: Camellia japonica is native to China and Japan. It is characterized by a slightly silvery trunk and foliage with leathery, dark green leaves. It can reach a height of 3 to 8 yards.

Flowering: From December to March abundant white, pink, or red or red flowers bloom.

Environment and exposure: It must be maintained throughout the year in a well-ventilated and bright place, possibly near a window. In summer it is possible to take it outside from March to September, placing it in an area of the penumbra. The preferable temperature in winter fluctuates between 6 and 12 degrees Celsius – 42-56 F..

Watering: Camellia needs constantly moist soil in summer, while in winter it can be watered more rarely.

Fertilization: It is recommended to fertilize in the period between flowering and the end of autumn, using liquid fertilizer every 2 weeks.

Repotting: It is necessary to repot in the spring, once every 2-4 years, cutting the roots.

Soil: The mixture must be 1/5 of clay, 2/5 of peat, and 2/5 of sand.

Pruning: Pruning the branches after flowering, reducing the number of leaves of the shoots to a number of 2 or 3.

Binding: The branches can always be tied, with the exception of the flowering ones. Sprouts, on the other hand, should only be tied towards the end of summer when they are better strengthened.

Multiplication: It is recommended by cuttings, although not always of sure success.

CHERRY OF THE ANTILLES (MALPIGHIA COCCIGERA)

Family: Malpighiaceae

Description: It is an evergreen shrub from the Antilles, the leaves, thorny, have a bright green color.

Blooming: In the period from June to August, it produces small pinkishwhite flowers.

Environment and exposure: Throughout the year it can be kept indoors, near a window, in a bright and ventilated place, however, it cannot stand the direct sun. In winter it is recommended to keep the temperature around 1820 degrees Celsius – 64-68 F..

Watering: Throughout the year it is best to keep the soil constantly humid. In fact, even in winter, the plant is kept in a warm environment

Fertilization: Throughout the year the fertilizer will be given once every two weeks, except in winter, when 4- weeks will pass between one administration and another.

Repotting: We recommend always repotting in the spring, once a year, or once every two years, popping up and cutting the roots.

Soil: The ideal soil consists of a mixture of 2/4 of clay, 1 / of peat and 1/4 of sand.

Pruning: The shoots must be pruned in order to reduce the number of leaves to one or two pairs, while the branches can always be pruned.

Binding: Branches and shoots can always be tied as long as they are strong enough not to risk breaking.

Multiplication: The plant is suitable for multiplication by cuttings or by seed.

CHINESE ELM (ULMUS PARVIFOLIA)

Family: ulmaceae

Description: it is a large tree from areas of China, it has a light-colored trunk and rather thin branches, rich in oval leaves, light green and shaped. If allowed to grow in its areas of origin, it reaches a height of twenty yards.

Environment and exposure: throughout the year it can be kept indoors, next to a bright and sunny window. For the summer period, it is advisable to take it outside, also placing it in the sun, if this is not too intense. In winter, given the great strength of the Elm, it can be kept both at warm temperatures (10-20 degrees celsius - 50-68 F.) and cooler (5-10 degrees celsius).

Watering: in summer it is good to water continuously and in abundance, avoiding that the soil remains too dry. During the winter, if it "winters in the heat", it will be watered as in summer, otherwise use more moderate and occasional doses of water, while keeping the soil moist.

Fertilization: for the entire period from March to September we recommend fertilizing once every 2 weeks. In winter the use of fertilizer will decrease to once every 4-5 weeks.

Repotting: repotting should be practiced once every two years, when spring arrives, sprouting and cutting the roots that have developed too much.

Soil: the ideal soil for growing Elm is made up of a mixture of 2/4 clay, 1/4 sand and 1/4 peat.

Pruning: branches and shoots can be pruned throughout the year. It is advisable to trim the shoots especially when they have reached 5-6 pairs of leaves, to shorten them to 2-3 pairs.

Binding: the metal wire should be applied only on the branches and on the shoots that are quite robust and lignified.

Multiplication: the easiest method is that of multiplication by cuttings.

CHRISTMAS STAR (EUPHORBIA PULCHERRIMA)

Family: euforbiaceae

Description: shrub native to Central America, characterized by a gnarled and rough trunk, vertical branches and light green lobed leaves.

Flowering: in winter reddish inflorescences develop.

Environment and exposure: the poinsettia should be placed in a bright and sunny area, but not exposed to drafts. In winter the recommended temperature is between 15 and 18 degrees Celsius – 59-64 F.

Watering: we recommend watering abundantly throughout the year, keeping the soil constantly humid.

Fertilization: fertilization should be practiced only in the period from March to October, distributing fertilizer once every 2/3 weeks.

Repotting: It is better to repot the Christmas star every year, in the months of March-April, cutting the roots and shortening those that have grown too long.

Soil: the most suitable mixture is made up of 2/5 clay, 2/5 peat and 1/5 sand.

Pruning: the poinsettia needs pruning of branches and shoots only in August.

Binding: given the structure of this plant, tying is not necessary.

Multiplication: methods of multiplication by seed and by cuttings are recommended.

CICAS (CYCAS REVOLUTA)

Family: Cicadaceae

Description: Palm-like plant, native to Japan and characterized by an unbranched stem and elongated dark green leaves erected by a shadow.

Environment and exposure: We recommend keeping it near a well-lit window throughout the year. During the winter the ideal temperature is between 10 and 15 degrees Celsius - 50-59 F..

Watering: Throughout the summer the watering must be abundant and regular; while more moderate doses are recommended during the winter.

Fertilization: For the period from March to September it is good to fertilize once every 2 weeks, with liquid fertilizer. In winter it is preferable to wait 4-5 weeks between one fertilization and another.

Repotting: For Cicas it is sufficient to practice repotting once every 4 or 5 years, cutting the roots and shortening those that are too long.

Soil: A mixture consisting of 1/4 clay, 1/4 peat and 2/4 of sand is recommended, being careful to prepare good drainage.

Pruning: Especially during the spring period it is good to cut the old leaves grown at the base of the stem.

Binding: given the somewhat particular nature of this plant, the binding is superfluous and therefore not recommended.

Multiplication: A good method for obtaining new plants is that of multiplication by seed.

CISSUS ANTARCTICA (CISSUS ANTARCTICA)

Family: Vitaceae

Description: It is an evergreen creeper, originally from Australia. It is characterized by rather rapid growth and a consequent abundance of branches and leaves, which are shaped and have a light green color.

Environment and exposure: Being a robust plant, it can adapt well to different temperatures. It is advisable to keep it, therefore, between 15 and 18 degrees Celsius – 59-64 F., in a fairly illuminated place, throughout the year.

Watering: Accustomed moderate watering, both in summer and in winter.

Fertilization: The period in which it needs more fertilization is from February to October when it can be fertilized once a week. During the winter stasis, it is sufficient to give fertilizer every 5-6 weeks.

Repotting: It is good to repot the still young plants, at least once a year in spring, given their fast growth. For the older ones, it is sufficient once every two years, always in the spring.

Soil: The ideal mixture consists of clay, peat and sand in the same temperatures, both hot and cool, requires proportions.

Pruning: During the vegetative phase it will be carried out frequently. We will have to decrease the number of leaves in the shoots to a number of two and eliminate the leaves that have grown too quickly.

Binding: Can be practiced throughout the year.

Multiplication: Cutting is recommended.

CORK OAK (QUERCUS SUBER)

Family: fagaceae

Description: it is an evergreen and very long-lived tree, native to the Mediterranean areas of Spain, France and Sardinia. It has a wrinkled trunk, silvery green and light green toothed leaves.

Environment and exposure: cork oak can be kept all year round next to a bright window, even if, during the summer it shows that it likes the outdoors and the sun. In winter temperatures between 10 and 15 degrees celsius - 5059 F. are recommended.

Watering: throughout the summer it is sufficient to keep the soil moist enough; during the winter you can decrease the dose of water, but without ever leaving the soil too dry.

Fertilization: it is necessary to fertilize only in the period between spring and autumn, by administering fertilizer every 2-3 weeks. In winter it is good to stop fertilizing.

Repotting: we recommend practicing repotting once every 2-3 years at the arrival of spring, cutting and shortening the roots.

Soil: to meet the needs of cork oak, the best composition of the soil is made up of soil, peat and sand in equal proportions.

Pruning: branches and shoots can be pruned throughout the year.

Binding: it is advisable to apply the wire only on well-lignified branches and shoots. The best time is summer.

Multiplication: for cork oak, the main methods of obtaining new seedlings are seed multiplication and layering.

CRASSULA ARBORESCENS (CRASSULA ARBORESCENS)

Family: Crassulaceae

Description: It is a tree from southern Africa with thick and fleshy green leaves. The trunk is dark but bright. It can reach a maximum height of 2-3 yards.

Environment and exposure: It can be at home next to a Juminosa window, but not in the sun, or outside from May to September in a shady place. The ideal temperature for winter is between 10 and 15 degrees Celsius – 50-59 F..

Watering: Being a plant that resists dry even for a month, it is best not to water it excessively. In summer, therefore, the watering will be moderate, and the interval times in winter will further expand.

Fertilization: In the period from May to September the liquid fertilizer will be supplied every month, while during the summer stasis the administration will stop.

Repotting: Once a year, cutting and shortening the roots. After repotting it is good not to water for 2 weeks.

Soil: The ideal soil is made up of 1/5 clay, peat for 2/5 and sand for 2/5.

Pruning: The branches can be pruned throughout the spring-summer period. The shoots must be sprouted when groups of leaves have formed, so as to leave only two or three pairs of leaves.

Binding: Can be done on branches and shoots throughout the year.

Multiplication: Excellent results can be obtained with the cutting method. The most suitable methods for obtaining new plants

CRYPTOMERIA (CRYPTOMERIA JAPONICA)

Family: taxodiaceae

Description: large conifer native to the forests of central Japan and southern China. It is characterized by a dark red bark, hanging branches and spiralshaped persistent leaves.

Environment and exposure: it is important to always keep it in a bright, dark place, without letting the sun hit it. For the winter the ideal temperature is between 8 and 15 degrees Celsius - 46-59 F.

Watering: throughout the year it is good to water abundantly and regularly, spraying the leaves two or three times a week.

Fertilization: fertilization must be applied for the entire period from March to October, with liquid fertilizer distributed once every 3-4 weeks.

Repotting: we recommend repotting Cryptomeria once every 3 or 4 years, in the months of March and April, shortening overgrown roots.

Soil: the most suitable mixture for the best development of the plant consists of 2/5 of clay, 1/5 of peat and 2/5 of sand.

Pruning: in spring it is recommended to prune the branches. The shoots, on the other hand, are topped both in spring and autumn, shortening them by 2/3.

Binding: for Cryptomeria March is the best time to tie branches and shoots, provided they are well lignified.

Multiplication: the most suitable methods for obtaining new plants are those by seed and by cutting.

DAISY (CHRYSANTHEMUM)

Family: composite

Description: it is a plant native to China, with numerous erect stems that can reach a height of 27-32 inch. The leaves are green and elongated.

Flowering: in the period between May and August, 2 inch diameter flowers with yellow central eye and white, yellow or purple petals appear on the lignified branches according to the various species.

Environment and exposure: all year round it can be kept in a very bright and sunny place. In summer it is recommended to stay outdoors, in the sun. The temperature at which it is good to keep it during the winter is around 15-18 degrees Celsius – 59-64 F.

Watering: the water should be given abundantly and regularly throughout, but especially in the summer.

Fertilization: the fertilizer must be supplied throughout the year except in the flowering period. From spring to autumn, a 2-3 weeks dose is recommended.

Repotting: we recommend repotting once every 2-3 years, when spring arrives, cutting and sprouting overgrown roots.

Soil: the ideal soil for growing daisy is made up of 2/5 clay, 2/5 peat and 1/5 sand.

Pruning: the most suitable period for pruning branches and shoots is at the end of flowering. Anticipating the operational risks that flowering will not take place.

Binding: slightly lignified branches and shoots can be tied, even if the application of the wire is often not necessary.

Multiplication: multiplication methods by seed are recommended every in winter one dose every 4-5 weeks. by cuttings.

DWARF ORANGE (FORTUNELLA HINDSII)

Family: Rutaceae

Description: It is a subtropical tree from eastern Asia and the Mediterranean area, characterized by small leaves and fruits.

Flowering: Dwarf orange will begin to give small and fragrant flowers only in adulthood.

Environment and exposure: All year round it can be kept indoors, in a bright and well-ventilated place. For the period from May to September, it can be placed outdoors in the sun or dim light. During the winter keep the temperature between 5 and 10 degrees Celsius - 41-50 F..

Watering: In summer it will be practiced often and in abundance. In winter it will be sufficient to water only when it is dry.

Fertilization: It is better to fertilize every 2 weeks in the summer. Increase the period in autumn and spring, until it stops in winter.

Repotting: This should be practiced every 2-3 years, at the beginning of spring, popping up and cutting the roots.

Soil: Good soil is made up of clay, peat and sand in equal proportions.

Pruning: Care must be taken to prune the branches because they do not grow back easily. The shoots must be cut to leave groups of 2-3 leaves.

Binding: Can be practiced on already robust and lignified branches and shoots.

Multiplication: The seed method is recommended

ERETHIA BUXIFOLIA (CARMONA MICROPHYLLA)

Family: boraginaceae

Description: it is an evergreen shrub from the tropical areas of southern China and south-east Asia. The trunk is of a silvery green color, and develops dark green oval leaves. In the period following flowering, the berries appear to change from green to red.

Flowering: from spring to summer white flowers bloom.

Environment and exposure: being a tropical plant, it is well suited to the internal temperatures of the house (15-24 degrees Celsius – 59-75 F.). It is always best to keep it in a bright place and not expose it to the sun. In the period between May and September it can be outside.

Watering: it is advisable to water abundantly throughout the year.

Fertilization: during the vegetative phase of greater intensity, between March and September, it is better to fertilize every 2 weeks with liquid fertilizer. In winter it is good to limit fertilization to once every 4 weeks.

Repotting: to be carried out always in spring and every two years, cutting and shortening the roots.

Soil: the recommended mixture is 2/5 of soil for bonsai, 2/5 of peat or May and September can be outside. "year. peat and 1/5

Pruning: the branches can always be pruned, while in the shoots the leaves will be decreased from groups of 6 or more to groups of 2 or 3.

Binding: you can apply the metal wire throughout the whole Sprouts can be tied only if they are strong and lignified enough

Multiplication: the method by cutting or by seed is recommended.

EUFORBIA (EUPHORBIA BALSAMIFERA)

Family: euphorbiaceae

Description: it is a cactaceous shrub native to West Africa which, like all plants in the family, has white latex inside, which comes out of any wounds on the trunk.

Environment and exposure: it can be at home next to a window all year round, in winter the temperature must remain between 10 and 15 degrees Celsius – 50-59 F. You can take it outside in summer without worrying too much about the sun, given its structure.

Watering: for the summer period it is sufficient to water once a week. During the winter, however, once every 2 weeks. When the plant begins to lose the leaves, you have to stop until they are reappeared.

Fertilization: to be practiced only in the period between May and September once a month.

Repotting: once a year in spring, shortening the roots. After repotting it is good not to water for 2 weeks.

Soil: the most suitable mixture consists of 1/5 of clay, 2/5 of sand and 2/5 of peat.

Pruning: it is better to prune branches and shoots between spring and summer. When latex comes out, it is better to dry it quickly, to avoid sticking.

Binding: it is not very suitable for this type of plant.

Multiplication: multiplications by cutting and by seeds are recommended.

FERN (GREVILLEA ROBUST)

Family: protaceae

Description: The tree fern is a tree with large flowers and broad, pinnate leaves, native to Western Australia.

Environment and exposure: it can be placed in front of a bright window, but not in the sun. In winter it is advisable to keep the temperature between 12 and 15 degrees Celsius – 53-59 F.

Watering: throughout the year it is best to water continuously to keep the soil always moist.

Fertilization: it must be fertilized only in the vegetative period and in summer, preferably using liquid fertilizer, once every two weeks.

Repotting: repotting must be practiced annually during the spring, sprouting and cutting the roots.

Soil: The most suitable mixture for tree fern is made up of 2/5 clay, 1/5 peat and 2/5 sand.

Pruning: the branches can be pruned throughout the year. It is good to trim the shoots, removing excess leaves and those that have become too large.

Binding: branches and shoots as long as they are strong enough for the metal wire.

Multiplication: multiplication by cutting or seed is recommended.

FICUS (RETUSA GINSENG)

Family: Moracee

Description: They can be found on every continent in the tropic regions.

Placement: The ficus is an indoor tree that does not endure frosty conditions. It can be kept outside in the summer as long as temperatures are above 60°F (15°C). It requires a lot of light, preferably full sunlight, so be sure not to place it in a shady location. The temperature should be kept relatively constant. Figs can endure low humidity due to their thick, waxy leaves, but they prefer higher humidity and need extremely high humidity to develop aerial roots.

Watering : The Ficus should be watered normally, which means it should be given water generously whenever the soil gets slightly dry. The Bonsai Ficus prefers room temperature soft water and it can tolerate occasional over, or underwatering. We advise daily misting to maintain humidity, but too much misting can create fungal problems. The warmer the placement of the fig during winter the more water it needs. If it's kept in a cooler place it only needs to be kept slightly moist.

Fertilizing : Fertilize every two weeks during summer, and every four weeks during winter if the growth doesn't stop. Liquid fertilizer can be used as well as organic fertilizer pellets.

Pruning: Regular pruning is necessary to retain the tree's shape. Prune back to 2 leaves after 6-8 leaves have grown. Leaf pruning (defoliation) can be used to reduce leaf size, as some Ficus Bonsai species normally grow large leaves. If a considerable thickening of the trunk is desired, the Ficus can be left to grow freely for one or two years. The strong cuts that are necessary afterward don't affect the Ficus' health and new shoots will grow from old wood. Larger wounds should be covered with cut paste

Wiring: Wiring and bending thin to medium Ficus branches is easy due to their flexibility, but you should check the wires regularly as they can cut into the bark very quickly. Strong branches should be shaped with guy-wires because they can be left on the tree for a much longer period.

Repotting: During the spring, every other year, using a basic Bonsai soil mixture. Ficus tolerates root-pruning very well.

Propagation: Cuttings can be planted at any time of the year, but they have the highest success rate during mid-summer growth. Air-layering will work best during spring, in April through May. In most cases, springtime is the best time for planting Ficus seeds.

Pests / diseases: Species are quite resistant against pests, but they are still susceptible to several issues depending on their location, and time of year, especially in the winter. Dry air and a lack of light weakens the Bonsai Ficus and often result in leaf drop. In poor conditions like these, they are sometimes infested with scale or spider mites. Placing customary insecticide sticks into the soil or spraying insecticide/miticide will get rid of the pests, but a weakened Ficus tree's living conditions must be improved. Using plant lamps 12 to 14 hours a day, and frequently misting the leaves will help in the recovery process.

Conclusion

Thank you again for purchasing this book. The art of keeping bonsais must be one of the most rewarding practices in the world today and even though it can take years of your life, it isn't something that you will ever regret doing. I hope it has given you a good idea of what is involved with starting a Bonsai tree.

If you have acquired a Bonsai tree, then you are ready for the next step. The true value in cultivating a Bonsai tree comes from the practice of caring for it, which is something that cannot easily be described. The practice of cultivating Bonsai trees is one full of intangible gifts that defy explanation.

As you care for your tree by monitoring its water intake, ensuring that it gets sufficient sunlight and watching it pass through the seasons you will also be molding it to match your inner vision of how you want it to look.

The time you spend with your tree as it slowly shifts from idea to reality will teach you many things about yourself and life in general. This is where the true value of practicing the art of Bonsai growing lies.

When pruning your Bonsai, remove everything that does not reflect your inner vision of how you want your tree to look.

Take a slow breath before making any cuts and try not to think about anything other than what you are doing. In doing this, you will come to see why this art form so enamored the Zen monks of ancient China and continues to captivate the imagination of millions of people the world over.

All of this will take practice and you are going to make mistakes, but that is the entire process of learning. Once you realize what you are capable of doing, you will want to do more and achieve more with growing these pieces of art.

This is a long journey that you are going to go on and even though it is one of growing trees in pots, it is more about self-discovery and it definitely is one that you are going to love to go on.